DISCARDED

The Early Modern Englishwoman:
A Facsimile Library of Essential Works

Series II

Printed Writings, 1641–1700: Part 2

Volume 5

Anne Killigrew

Selected and Introduced by
Patricia Hoffmann

General Editors
Betty S. Travitsky and Anne Lake Prescott

Coordinating Editor for this Volume
Robert C. Evans

The Introductory Note copyright © Patricia Hoffmann 2003

All rights reserved. No part of this publication may be reproduced, stored in a retrieval system, or transmitted in any form or by any means, electronic, mechanical, photocopying, recording, or otherwise without the prior permission of the publisher.

Published by
Ashgate Publishing Limited
Gower House
Croft Road
Aldershot
Hants GU11 3HR
England

Ashgate Publishing Company
Suite 420
101 Cherry Street
Burlington, VT 05401–4405
USA

Ashgate website: http://www.ashgate.com

British Library Cataloguing-in-Publication Data
Killigrew, Anne
  Anne Killigrew. - (The early modern Englishwoman : a
  facsimile library of essential works. Printed writings
  1641-1700, series 2 ; pt. 2, v. 5)
  I.Title II.Hoffmann, Patricia III.Evans, Robert C.
  821.4

Library of Congress Cataloging-in-Publication Data
The early modern Englishwoman: a facsimile library of essential works. Part 2. Printed Writings 1641–1700 / general editors, Betty S. Travitsky and Anne Lake Prescott.

Library of Congress Control Number: 2003100278

The image reproduced on the title page and on the case is taken from the frontispiece portrait in *Poems, By the Most Deservedly Admired Mrs. Katherine Philips* (1667). Reproduced by permission of the Folger Shakespeare Library, Washington, DC.

ISBN 0 7546 3097 8

Printed in Great Britain by Antony Rowe Ltd, Chippenham, Wiltshire.

CONTENTS

Preface by the General Editors

Introductory Note

Poems by Mrs Anne Killigrew

PREFACE
BY THE GENERAL EDITORS

Until very recently, scholars of the early modern period have assumed that there were no Judith Shakespeares in early modern England. Much of the energy of the current generation of scholars has been devoted to constructing a history of early modern England that takes into account what women actually wrote, what women actually read, and what women actually did. In so doing the masculinist representation of early modern women, both in their own time and ours, is deconstructed. The study of early modern women has thus become one of the most important—indeed perhaps the most important—means for the rewriting of early modern history.

The Early Modern Englishwoman: A Facsimile Library of Essential Works is one of the developments of this energetic reappraisal of the period. As the names on our advisory board and our list of editors testify, it has been the beneficiary of scholarship in the field, and we hope it will also be an essential part of that scholarship's continuing momentum.

The Early Modern Englishwoman is designed to make available a comprehensive and focused collection of writings in English from 1500 to 1750, both by women and for and about them. The three series of *Printed Writings* (1500–1640, 1641–1700, and 1701–1750) provide a comprehensive if not entirely complete collection of the separately published writings by women. In reprinting these writings we intend to remedy one of the major obstacles to the advancement of feminist criticism of the early modern period, namely the limited availability of the very texts upon which the field is based. The volumes in the facsimile library reproduce carefully chosen copies of these texts, incorporating significant variants (usually in appendices). Each text is preceded by a short introduction providing an overview of the life and work of a writer along with a survey of important scholarship. These works, we strongly believe, deserve a large readership—of historians, literary critics, feminist critics, and non-specialist readers.

The Early Modern Englishwoman also includes separate facsimile series of *Essential Works for the Study of Early Modern Women* and of *Manuscript Writings*. These facsimile series are complemented by *The Early Modern Englishwoman 1500–1750: Contemporary Editions*. Also under our general editorship, this series will include both old-spelling and modernized editions of works by and about women and gender in early modern England.

New York City
2003

INTRODUCTORY NOTE

That almost nothing is known of Anne Killigrew (1660–1685), the woman, the person, seems both strange and predictable. Strange because she was so well-connected to court (the poet laureate wrote an ode to her memory after all); strange also because her kinsmen and women of many generations were both court-connected and much commented upon. Her great grandfather, Sir William Killigrew (d. 1622) was given Hanworth, the estate near Hampton Court that became Anne Killigrew's family seat, by Elizabeth I. Her grandfather, Sir Robert Killigrew (c. 1579–1633), was knighted by James I. Her father, Dr. (of Divinity) Henry Killigrew (1612–1700), was Master of the Savoy (a palace rebuilt and endowed by Henry the Seventh as a hospital) after the Restoration, was also one of the prebendaries of Westminster, and was Chaplain and Almoner to James, Duke of York. An uncle, Sir William Killigrew (1605–1695), served at court for twenty-two years. Another uncle, Robert Killigrew (1610?–?), was gentleman of the privy chamber to Charles II, and served eventually in that same capacity to William and Mary and later to Queen Anne. Her aunt Anne, about whom the author Anne Killigrew wrote a poem, was until her death in 1641 dresser for Queen Henrietta Maria. Another aunt, Elizabeth Killigrew (1622–1680), was mistress of Charles II, by whom she had a daughter – Charlotte Killigrew. Anne Killigrew's most famous relative, at least from a literary standpoint, was the dramatist and court favourite Thomas Killigrew (1612–1683), unofficial jester to Charles II. During Anne Killigrew's lifetime most of her known living relatives were connected to the court. Some, like her cousin Henry Killigrew (1637–1705), first son of Thomas Killigrew, banished from court and brought back several times, were rogues; some, like her cousin Roger Killigrew (born c. 1663), Thomas Killigrew's youngest son and water bailiff of the Thames, were minor functionaries, serving at the court's behest. Anne Killigrew, related to many, was remarked on by none – until her death, and then perhaps at her father's request.

That nothing is known of Anne Killigrew may be predictable as well. She died young, perhaps too young to have been much noticed. We do know that Anne Killigrew was born in 1660 in St. Martin's Lane, London; that she is said, by George Ballard in *Memoirs Of Several Ladies* (1775), to have had 'a polite education' (p. 337), the exact definition of which is unknown; that she served as maid of honor to Mary of Modena, although her exact tenure at court is not known; and that she died of smallpox on June 16, 1685. We know that she wrote poetry, some of which her father collected and had published after her death. We know that she was buried in St. John the Baptist Chapel at the Savoy. We know that she painted. Her own poems include works about three of her paintings, and Dryden gives in his ode to her memory some vivid descriptions of her art work and its bosky scenes. Most of her history is lost; most of her paintings are lost; and probably much of her poetry is lost as well.

As it stands, anyone looking up Anne Killigrew in *The Oxford Companion to English Literature* (1932) would suspect that she was not a poet at all, but a title: 'Mrs. Anne, Ode to the Memory of, see Dryden'. The ode by Dryden (1631–1700) is famous; Anne Killigrew was, thereby, famous as well, but her fame came via naked nomination. Little was, or is, known of her poetry, less of her life; no edition beyond the 1967 Scholars' Facsimiles & Reprints' Killigrew edited by Richard Morton has been done, and he provides only four notes, all of which are on the proper names and titles of Killigrew's 'friends and relatives [who] appear in the volume' (p. x). The general assumption has been that Dryden's ode on Anne Killigrew is hyperbolic, that he wrote overweening praise to salve a father's grief and to serve as an accommodation to a well-connected family; after all, many a Killigrew was a Dryden friend. Killigrew, herself, however, would have condemned currying favor; indeed she does: 'O, the Laurel'd Fool!' she says, 'who can accept for Pay / Of what he does, what others say' ('The Discontent', stanza IV).

Poems by Mrs. Anne Killgrew (1686).

We do have twenty-five extant completed poems and five fragments by Anne Killigrew – all collected and published by her father soon after her death. That there was probably more poetry seems fairly clear. The several occasional poems and epigrams seem to suggest a poet quite conversant with the period's propensity to comment and compliment in verse. Since she did one poem 'On the Birth-day of Queen Katherine', it does not seem far beyond the realm of belief that she might have noted the king's birthday in verse, or her father's – or her uncle's, come to that. Her poem 'To My Lord Colrane, *In Answer to his Complemental Verses sent me under the Name of* CLEANOR' certainly suggests that she was at least somewhat involved in coterie 'conversations'. Killigrew is often witty – as in 'On Galla', for instance, in which Killigrew's 'we' and 'one' deliciously imply a coterie of Corinnas discussing bitter Galla and her toilette. Can a young woman at court, capable of 'On Galla', forget the joy of such satire and never sting again? Killigrew says of the pimply Katherine Philips (in '*Upon the saying that my* Verses *were made by another*') that she 'Ow'd not her Glory to a Beauteous Face' – a witty way to say this, even if she isn't being snide. One wonders if her more biting table talk, like Coleridge's, was suppressed by a family editor. Too, twenty-five completed poems seem few for a woman who might have been writing poetry since she was in her early teens, especially for a woman whose first attempt at verse, if the note in her published edition can be believed, is an epic: '*This* [Killigrew's fragment, 'Alexandreis'] *was the first Essay of this young Lady in Poetry, but finding the Task she had undertaken hard, she laid it by till Practice and more time should make her equal to so great a Work*' (p. 5).

Killigrew's work itself suggests lacunae in her development. For instance, Killigrew's metrics are often predictable, and she writes invariably in couplets, uses almost invariably masculine rhyme, and invariably iambic pentameter or tetrameter, rising at most to the inevitable substituted foot, a trochee. Although she once, in 'A Pastoral Dialogue' ('Stay gentle Nymph, nor so solic'tous be'), manages to split one line of iambic pentameter between two speakers and to add an odd and isolated aposiopesis (or sudden interruption), her metrical rigidity is consistent; each of her twenty-five completed poems is either all pentameter (eighteen) or all tetrameter (six), offering nary a blending. Then suddenly there is 'The Discontent', possibly her latest poem. Kicking up her feet, she sprinkles in lines of trimeter, hexameter, even a line of dimeter and a line of octameter, making this poem metrically her most ambitious. 'The Discontent' shows metrical virtuosity of the sort Alexander Pope (1688–1744) will later play with in his 'Essay on Criticism' (1711). However, in Killigrew's case no clear evolution is evident; there seem to be missing links.

The poems that we do have suggest a sometimes conventional, sometimes merely competent, but often quite promising poet, and an English one. Unlike many of her contemporaries (including many of the women whose work was published in the period) Killigrew never uses a word of Latin, or French, or Italian. In many other ways, however, she is a woman of her own time. Killigrew, like other religious poets of her day, often uses Biblical allusion to point out the relationship between the Old Testament and contemporary history. She, like her pre-Augustan, post-metaphysical contemporaries, uses classical allusion as equivalents to the biblical: Killigrew is Cassandra in '*Upon the saying that my* Verses *were made by another*' (a poet who speaks the truth, but who is believed too late); meanwhile, Lady Berkeley in 'To my Lady Berkeley, Afflicted upon her Son, My Lord Berkeley's Early Engaging in the Sea-Service' becomes Penelope, the 'Ithacesian Queen', and her son, Lord Berkeley, becomes Telemachus. Indeed, Killigrew would have been a fine eighteenth-century poet, as elements of what would later be called Augustan poetry are already obvious in her work; she writes exclusively in couplets, equates England with Rome, and invokes the classical heroes of Ovid and Virgil, as well as the help of their muse: 'If thou O Muse wilt thy assistance give, / Such as made Naso and great Maro live …' ('Alexandreis').

Germaine Greer in the Introduction to *Kissing the Rod: An Anthology of Seventeenth-Century Women's Verse* (1988) says that she and her coeditors will 'be best pleased if … our book is superseded by … studies of more depth and discrimination, prompted in part by our efforts' (p. 31). Kate Lilley says in her introduction to Margaret Cavendish's work that her [i.e., Lilley's] 'role as editor and introducer adds another level to this [Cavendish's and her reader's] recursive process of female collaboration' and that her [Lilley's] collection and edition 'solicits new readers and new readings' (p. xxix). Perhaps it is the role of 'introducer' of newly reclaimed work that makes this urging for further readings so ubiquitous with the editors of early modern women authors. There is, after all, no way to make up for decades of critical neglect in one edition, by one editor. We can only hope for the dialogue to begin.

Thirty-five copies of the posthumous (1685/6) edition of Anne Killigrew's *Poems* survive: 24 in the USA; 8 in England; 2 in Australia; 1 in Canada; 1 in New Zealand; the copy held at the Folger Shakespeare Library is reproduced here, while the copy held at the Alexander Turnbull Library, Wellington, New Zealand is the copy reproduced for the 1967 Morton Scholars' Facsimiles & Reprints Edition. The Folger Shakespeare Library's copy of *Poems* was chosen for this facsimile edition both because of its condition (sound and legible) and its provenance. This copy has the bookplate of Henry Lord Colerane ('The right Hon/ble Henry Lord Colerane in y/e Kingdom of Ireland 1702'), strongly suggesting that this copy was originally owned by the man to whom Anne Killigrew wrote her 'TO My Lord Colrane, *In Answer to his Complemental Verses sent me under the Name of* CLEANOR'. Colrane (variously Coleraine, Colerane, and Colraine), the antiquary Henry Hare, Baron Coleraine (1636–1708), wrote a history of Tottenham High Cross, *The Situation Of Paradise Found Out: Being An History Of A Late Pilgrimage Unto The Holy Land, With A Necessary Apparatus Prefixt, Giving Light Into The Whole Design* (1683), the book that may have begun the poetical conversation between him and Anne Killigrew, and has sometimes had *Plaine English, Or, An Discourse Concerning The Accommodation, The Armie, The Association* (1643), a short book on the civil war, attributed to him. John Playford's *Vade Mecum* (1696) is dedicated to him.

The Folger copy shows interesting signs of peculiar sorts of reader-response. Thus, various marginal markings (including x's, horizontal lines, and vertical lines) have been added throughout the text, two lines of verse are crossed through (but are still plainly legible) on page 29, and the word 'quarrels' on page 84 has been replaced with the inked-in words 'but broils'.

Acknowledgements

This book is dedicated to Ann Blaisdell Tracy, friend, and mentor to me always; T. Eric and Greta Hoffmann, loves of my life; Candace and River Hoffmann, extensions of my world; Agostino Pandozy, who gave me real pearls; and Shirley Tolley Nock, who started it all.

References

Wing K442

Barash, Carol (1989), 'Augustan Women's Mythmaking: English Women Writers and the Body of Monarchy, 1660–1720', Ph.D. dissertation, Princeton University

— (1996), *English Women's Poetry, 1649–1714; Politics, Community, and Linguistic Authority*, Oxford: Clarendon

Day, Robert Adams (1980), 'Muses in the Mud: the Female Wits Anthropologically Considered', *Women's Studies* (7)

Eaton, Claribel R. (1931), 'The Poems of Anne Killigrew', MA Thesis, George Washington University

Ezell, Margaret (1993), *Writing Women's Literary History*, Baltimore: Johns Hopkins University Press

Fraser, Antonia (1984), *The Weaker Vessel*, NY: Knopf

Gillespie, Stuart (1996), 'Another Pindaric Ode: "To the Pious Memory of Mrs Ann Killigrew"', *Restoration* (20)

Greer, Germaine, Susan Hastings, Jeslyn Medoff, and Melinda Sansone (eds) (1989), *Kissing the Rod: An Anthology of Seventeenth-Century Women's Verse*, NY: Farrar Straus Giroux

Hobby, Elaine (1989), *Virtue of Necessity: English Women's Writing 1649–88*, Ann Arbor: University of Michigan Press

Hoffmann, Patricia (1995), 'Anne Killigrew (1660–1685): Twenty-five Poems', Ph.D. dissertation, State University of New York at Albany

Morton, Richard (ed.) (1967), *Poems by Mrs. Anne Killigrew. 1686* Gainesville, FL: Scholars' Facsimiles & Reprints

Ockerbloom, Mary Mark (ed) (2000), *A Celebration of Women Writers*, Online at http://digital.library.upenn.edu/women/killigrew

Rex, Michael Charles (1993), 'The Woman's Voice: Experiments of Genre in the Poetry of Anne Killigrew', MA Thesis, Texas & M University

— (1995), 'Education for Women? Get Serious: A Look at the Argument for Women's Education in Writings of Anne Killigrew, Mary Astell, Mary Pix, and Mary, Lady Chudleigh', *Proceedings of the Third Dakotas Conference on Earlier British Literature*

Reynolds, Myra (1920), *The Learned Lady in England 1650–1760*, Boston: Houghton-Mifflin

Stanford, Ann (ed) 1972), *The Women Poets in English: An Anthology*, NY: Herder and Herder

Stevenson, Jane and Peter Davidson (eds) (2001), *Early Modern Women Poets (1520–1700): An Anthology*, Oxford: Oxford University Press

Straub, Kristina (1987), 'Indecent Liberties with a Poet: Audience and the Metaphor of Rape in Killigrew's "Upon the Saying That My Verses Were Made by Another" and Pope's "Arbothnot"', *Tulsa Studies in Women's Literature* (6)

Todd, Janet (1989), *The Sign of Angelica: Women, Writing and Fiction 1660–1800*, NY: Columbia University Press

Wheeler, David (1998), 'Beyond Art: Reading Dryden's Anne Killigrew in its Political Moment', *South Central Review* (15)

PATRICIA HOFFMANN

Poems by Mrs. Anne Killigrew (Wing K442) is reproduced, by permission, from the copy in the Folger Shakespeare Library (shelfmark K442 Cage). The book is a quarto volume with a text block size of 184 cm × 110 cm. In the Folger copy, as in other copies of Killigrew's poems, pages 68 and 69 are misnumbered as 60 and 61. Normal pagination then resumes with 70–71. However, the expected pages 72 and 73 are missing: the numbering jumps from 71 to 74, although there is no break in the sense of the text at this point. On page 24 of the Folger copy, the word 'Ithacensian' has been partially obscured.

Places where the text is difficult to read:

99.6 yet

Mrs Anne Killigrew.
Painted by her self   I. Beckett fec:

POEMS

BY

Mrs Anne Killigrew.

Immodicis brevis est ætas, & rara Senectus.
Mart. l. 6. Ep. 29.

These POEMS are Licensed to be Published,
Sept. 30. 1685.

Ro. L'Estrange.

LONDON:
Printed for *Samuel Lowndes*, over against *Exeter Exchange* in
the *Strand.* 1686.

[ ]

THE PUBLISHER TO THE READER.

Reader, dost ask, What Work we here display?
What fair and Novel Piece salutes the Day?
Know, that a Virgin bright this POEM writ,
A *Grace* for Beauty, and a *Muse* for Wit!
Who, when none higher in *Loves* Courts might sway,
Despis'd the Mertile, for the nobler Bay!
Nor could *Apollo* or *Minerva* tell,
Whither her Pen or Pencil did excel!

But while these Pow'rs laid both to her their Claime,
Behold, a Matron of a Heavenly Frame,
Antique, but Great and Comely in her Meen,
Upon whose gorgeous Robe inscrib'd was seen
Divine Vertue, took her from both away,
And thus with Anger and Disdain did say,
Of Me she Learn'd, with You she did but Play.

To

[ ]

To the Pious Memory
Of the Accomplisht Young LADY
Mrs Anne Killigrew,
Excellent in the two Sister-Arts of Poësie, and Painting.

An ODE.

I.

THou Youngest Virgin-Daughter of the Skies,
    Made in the last Promotion of the Blest;
  Whose Palmes, new pluckt from Paradise,
In spreading Branches more sublimely rise,
Rich with Immortal Green above the rest:
Whether, adopted to some Neighbouring Star,
Thou rol'st above us, in thy wand'ring Race,
  Or, in Procession fixt and regular,
  Mov'd with the Heavens Majestick Pace;
  Or, call'd to more Superiour Bliss,
Thou tread'st, with Seraphims, the vast Abyss.

[ ]

What ever happy Region be thy place,
Cease thy Celestial Song a little space;
(Thou wilt have Time enough for Hymns Divine,
   Since Heav'ns Eternal Year is thine.)
Hear then a Mortal Muse thy Praise rehearse,
     In no ignoble Verse;
But such as thy own voice did practise here,
When thy first Fruits of Poesie were giv'n;
To make thy self a welcome Inmate there:
   While yet a young Probationer,
   And Candidate of Heav'n.

II.

If by Traduction came thy Mind,
Our Wonder is the less to find.
A Soul so charming from a Stock so good;
Thy Father was transfus'd into thy Blood:
So wert thou born into the tuneful strain,
(An early, rich, and inexhausted Vain.)
   But if thy Præexisting Soul
   Was form'd, at first, with Myriads more,
It did through all the Mighty Poets roul,

Who *Greek* or *Latine* Laurels wore.
And was that *Sappho* laſt, which once it was before.
 If ſo, then ceaſe thy flight, *O Heav'n-born Mind!*
 Thou haſt no Droſs to purge from thy Rich Ore,
 Nor can thy Soul a fairer Manſion find,
 Than was the Beauteous Frame ſhe left behind:
Return, to fill or mend the Quire, of thy Celeſtial kind.

III.

May we preſume to ſay, that at thy Birth,
New joy was ſprung in Heav'n, as well as here on Earth.
 For ſure the Milder Planets did combine
 On thy Auſpicious Horoſcope to ſhine,
 And ev'n the moſt Malicious were in Trine.
  Thy Brother-Angels at thy Birth
  Strung each his Lyre, and tun'd it high,
  That all the People of the Skie
  Might know a Poeteſs was born on Earth.
   And then if ever, Mortal Ears
   Had heard the Muſick of the Spheres!
   And if no cluſt'ring Swarm of Bees
 On thy ſweet Mouth diſtill'd their golden Dew,

'Twas that, such vulgar Miracles,
Heav'n had not Leasure to renew:
For all the Blest Fraternity of Love
Solemniz'd there thy Birth, and kept thy Holyday above.

IV.

O Gracious God! How far have we
Prophan'd thy Heav'nly Gift of Poesy?
Made prostitute and profligate the Muse,
Debas'd to each obscene and impious use,
Whose Harmony was first ordain'd Above
For Tongues of Angels, and for Hymns of Love?
O wretched We! why were we hurry'd down
    This lubrique and adult'rate age,
      (Nay added fat Pollutions of our own)
    T'increase the steaming Ordures of the Stage?
What can we say t'excuse our *Second Fall?*
Let this thy *Vestal*, Heav'n, attone for all!
Her *Arethusian* Stream remains unsoil'd,
Unmixt with Forreign Filth, and undefil'd,
Her Wit was more than Man, her Innocence a Child!

V.

Art she had none, yet wanted: anon
For Nature did that Want supply,
So rich in Treasures of her Own,
She might our boasted Stores defy:
Such Noble Vigour did her Verse adorn,
That it seem'd borrow'd, where 'twas only born.
Her Morals too were in her Bosome bred
By great Examples daily fed,
What in the best of Books, her Fathers Life, she read.
And to be read her self she need not fear,
Each Test, and ev'ry Light, her Muse will bear,
Though *Epictetus* with his Lamp were there.
Ev'n Love (for Love sometimes her Muse exprest)
Was but a *Lambent-flame* which play'd about her Brest:
Light as the Vapours of a Morning Dream,
So cold herself, whilst she such Warmth exprest,
'Twas *Cupid* bathing in *Diana*'s Stream.

VI.

Born to the Spacious Empire of the *Nine*,
One would have thought, she should have been content
To manage well that Mighty Government:
But what can young ambitious Souls confine?
    To the next Realm she stretcht her Sway,
    For *Painture* neer adjoyning lay,
A plenteous Province, and alluring Prey.
A Chamber of Dependences was fram'd,
(As Conquerors will never want Pretence,
    When arm'd, to justifie the Offence.)
And the whole Fief, in right of Poetry she claim'd.
    The Country open lay without Defence:
For Poets frequent In-rodes there had made,
    And perfectly could represent
The Shape, the Face, with ev'ry Lineament;
And all the large Demains which the *Dumb-Sister* sway'd,
    All bow'd beneath her Government,
    Receiv'd in Triumph wheresoe're she went.
Her Pencil drew, what e're her Soul design'd,
And oft the happy Draught surpass'd the Image in her Mind.

The

[ ]

The *Sylvan* Scenes of Herds and Flocks,
And fruitful Plains and barren Rocks,
Of shallow Brooks that flow'd so clear,
The Bottom did the Top appear;
Of deeper too and ampler Flouds,
Which as in Mirrors, shew'd the Woods;
Of lofty Trees with Sacred Shades,
And Perspectives of pleasant Glades,
Where Nymphs of brightest Form appear,
And shaggy Satyrs standing neer,
Which them at once admire and fear.
The Ruines too of some Majestick Piece,
Boasting the Pow'r of ancient *Rome* or *Greece*,
Whose Statues, Freezes, Columns broken lie,
And though deface't, the Wonder of the Eie,
What Nature, Art, bold Fiction e're durst frame,
Her forming Hand gave Shape unto the Name.
So strange a Concourse ne're was seen before,
But when the peopl'd Ark the whole Creation bore.

VII.

VII.

The Scene then chang'd, with bold Erected Look
Our Martial King the Eye with Reverence strook:
For not content t'express his Outward Part,
Her hand call'd out the Image of his Heart,
His Warlike Mind, his Soul devoid of Fear,
His High-designing Thoughts, were figur'd there,
As when, by Magick, Ghosts are made appear.

Our Phenix Queen was portrai'd too so bright,
Beauty alone could Beauty take so right:
Her Dress, her Shape, her matchless Grace,
Were all observ'd, as well as heav'nly Face.
With such a Peerless Majesty she stands,
As in that Day she took from Sacred hands
The Crown; 'mong num'rous Heroins was seen,
More yet in Beauty, than in Rank, the Queen!

Thus nothing to her *Genius* was deny'd,
But like a Ball of Fire the further thrown,
   Still with a greater Blaze she shone,
And her bright Soul broke out on ev'ry side.

[ ]

What next she had design'd, Heaven only knows,
To such Immod'rate Growth her Conquest rose,
That Fate alone their Progress could oppose.

VIII.

Now all those Charmes, that blooming Grace,
The well-proportion'd Shape, and beauteous Face,
Shall never more be seen by Mortal Eyes;
In Earth the much lamented Virgin lies!
  Not Wit, nor Piety could Fate prevent;
  Nor was the cruel *Destiny* content
  To finish all the Murder at a Blow,
  To sweep at once her Life, and Beauty too;
But, like a hardn'd Fellon, took a pride
      To work more Mischievously flow,
      And plunder'd first, and then destroy'd.
O double Sacriledge on things Divine,
To rob the Relique, and deface the Shrine!
    But thus *Orinda* dy'd:
  Heav'n, by the same Disease, did both translate,
As equal were their Souls, so equal was their Fate.

IX.

IX.

Mean time her Warlike Brother on the Seas
His waving Streamers to the Winds displays,
And vows for his Return, with vain Devotion, pays.
    Ah, Generous Youth, that Wish forbear,
    The Winds too soon will waft thee here!
    Slack all thy Sailes, and fear to come,
Alas, thou know'st not, Thou art wreck'd at home!
No more shalt thou behold thy Sister's Face,
Thou hast already had her last Embrace.
But look aloft, and if thou ken'st from far,
Among the *Pleiad*'s a New-kindl'd Star,
If any sparkles, than the rest, more bright,
'Tis she that shines in that propitious Light.

X.

When in mid-Aire, the Golden Trump shall sound,
    To raise the Nations under ground;
    When in the Valley of *Jehosaphat*,
The Judging God shall close the Book of Fate;
    And there the last Assizes keep,
    For those who Wake, and those who Sleep;

When

[ ]

When ratling Bones together fly,
From the four Corners of the Skie,
When Sinews o're the Skeletons are spread,
Those cloath'd with Flesh, and Life inspires the Dead;
The Sacred Poets first shall hear the Sound,
  And formost from the Tomb shall bound:
For they are cover'd with the lightest Ground
And streight, with in-born Vigour, on the Wing,
Like mounting Larkes, to the New Morning sing.
There *Thou*, Sweet Saint, before the Quire shalt go,
As Harbinger of Heav'n, the Way to show,
The Way which thou so well haft learn'd below.

J. Dryden.

[ ]

The Epitaph
Engraved on her TOMB.

P. M. S.
Annæ Killigrew,
Doctoris KILLIGREW Filiæ,
Quæ in ipso Ætatis flore Obiit.
JUNII 16. 1685.

Heu jacet, fato victa,
    Quæ stabat ubique victrix
Forma, ingenio, religione ;
Plura collegerat in se Unâ,
Quàm vel sparsa mireris in omnibus !
Talem quis pingat, nisi penicillo quod tractavit ?

Aut

[   ]

Aut quis canat, nisi Poëta sui similis?
  Cum tanta sciret, hoc Unum ignoravit,
    Quanta, nempe, esset;
      Aut si norit,
    Mirare Modestiam,
Tantis incorruptam dotibus.
Laudes meruisse satis illi fuit,
Has ne vel audiret, laudatores omnes fugerat,
  Contenta paterno Lare,
Dum & sibi Aula patebat adulatrix.
  Mundum sapere an potuit,
  Quæ ab infantia Christum sapuerat?
    Non modo semper Virgo,
  Sed & virginum Exemplar.
    Gentis suæ Decus,
      Ævi Splendor,
    Sexus Miraculum.
  Nullâ Vertute inferior cuiquam,
    Cuilibet superior multâ.
  Optimi Deliciæ patris,
Etiam numerosâ optimâque prole fortunatissimi:
  Priorem tamen invidit nemo,

[   ]

(Seu frater, seu soror)
Quin potius coluere omnes, omnibus suavem & officiosam,
Amorisque commune Vinculum & Centrum.
Vix ista credes, Hanc si nescieris;
Credet majora, qui scierit.

Abi Viator, & Plange:
Si eam plangi oporteat,
Cui, tam piè morienti,
Vel Cœlites planserint.

———————————————

The

The same
Turned into English.

BY Death, alas, here Conquer'd lies,
She who from All late bore the Prize
In Beauty, Wit, Vertue Divine:
In whom those Graces did combine,
Which we admir'd in others see,
When they but singly scatter'd be!

Who her, *so Great*, can paint beside,
The Pencil her own Hand did guide?
What Verse can celebrate her Fame,
But such as She herself did frame?

Though much Excellence she did show,
And many Qualities did know,
Yet this, alone, she could not tell,
To wit, *How much she did excel.*

[ ]

Or if her Worth she rightly knew,
More to her Modesty was due,
That Parts in her no Pride could raise
Desirous still to merit Praise,
But fled, as she deserv'd, the Bays.
Contented always to retire,
Court Glory she did not admire;
Although it lay so neer and faire,
It's Grace to none more open were:
But with the World how should she close,
Who *Christ* in her first Childhood chose?

So with her Parents she did live,
That they to Her did Honour give,
As she to them. In a Num'rous Race
And Vertuous, the highest Place
None envy'd her: Sisters, Brothers
Her Admirers were and Lovers:
She was to all s'obliging sweet,
All in One Love to her did meet;
A Virgin-Life not only led,
But it's Example might be said

[a]

The

[ ]

The Ages Ornament, the Name
That gave her Sex and Country Fame.

  Those who her Person never knew,
Will hardly think these things are true:
But those that did, will More believe,
And higher things of her conceive.

  Thy Eyes in tears now, Reader, steep:
For Her if't lawful be to weep,
Whose blessed and Seraphique End
Angels in Triumph did attend.

ALEX-

Alexandreis.

I Sing the Man that never Equal knew,
Whose Mighty Arms all *Asia* did subdue,
Whose Conquests through the spacious World do ring,
That City-Raser, King-destroying King,
Who o're the Warlike *Macedons* did Reign,
And worthily the Name of *Great* did gain.
This is the Prince (if Fame you will believe,
To ancient Story any credit give.)
Who when the Globe of Earth he had subdu'd,
With Tears the easie Victory pursu'd;
Because that no more Worlds there were to win,
No further Scene to act his Glorys in.

Ah that some pitying *Muse* would now inspire
My frozen style with a Poetique fire,
And Raptures worthy of his Matchless Fame,
Whose Deeds I sing, whose never fading Name

Long as the world shall fresh and deathless last,
No less to future Ages, then the past.
Great my presumption is, I must confess,
But if I thrive, my Glory's ne're the less;
Nor will it from his Conquests derogate
A Female Pen his Acts did celebrate.
If thou O *Muse* wilt thy assistance give,
Such as made *Naso* and great *Maro* live,
With him whom *Melas* fertile Banks did bear,
Live, though their Bodies dust and ashes are;
Whose Laurels were not fresher, than their Fame
Is now, and will for ever be the same.
If the like favour thou wilt grant to me,
O Queen of Verse, I'll not ungrateful be,
My choicest hours to thee I'll Dedicate,
'Tis thou shalt rule, 'tis thou shalt be my Fate.
But if Coy Goddess thou shalt this deny,
And from my humble suit disdaining fly,
I'll stoop and beg no more, since I know this,
Writing of him, I cannot write amiss:
His lofty Deeds will raise each feeble line,
And God-like Acts will make my Verse Divine.

'Twas

'Twas at the time the golden Sun doth rise,
And with his Beams enlights the azure skies,
When lo a Troop in Silver Arms drew near,
The glorious Sun did nere so bright appear;
Dire Scarlet Plumes adorn'd their haughty Crests,
And crescent Shields did shade their shining Brests;
Down from their shoulders hung a Panthers Hide,
A Bow and Quiver ratled by their side;
Their hands a knotty well try'd Speare did bear,
Jocund they seem'd, and quite devoyd of fear.
These warlike Virgins were, that do reside
Near *Thermodons* smooth Banks and verdant side,
The Plains of *Themiscyre* their Birth do boast,
Thalestris now did head the beauteous Host;
She emulating that Illustrious Dame,
Who to the aid of *Troy* and *Priam* came,
And her who the *Retulian* Prince did aid,
Though dearly both for their Assistance paid.
But fear she scorn'd, nor the like fate did dread,
Her Host she often to the field had lead,
As oft in Triumph had return'd again,
Glory she only sought for all her pain.

This Martial Queen had heard how lowdly fame,
Eccho'd our Conquerors redoubted Name,
Her Soul his Conduct and his Courage fir'd,
To see the Heroe she so much admir'd;
And to *Hyrcania* for this cause she went,
Where *Alexander* (wholly then intent
On Triumphs and such Military sport)
At Truce with War held both his Camp and Court.
And while before the Town she did attend
Her Messengers return, she saw ascend
A cloud of Dust, that cover'd all the skie,
And still at every pause there stroke her eye.
The interrupted Beams of Burnisht Gold,
As dust the Splendour hid, or did unfold;
Loud Neighings of the Steeds, and Trumpets sound
Fill'd all the Air, and eccho'd from the ground:
The gallant *Greeks* with a brisk March drew near,
And their great Chief did at their Head appear.
And now come up to th'*Amazonian* Band,
They made a Hault and a respectful Stand:
And both the Troops (with like amazement strook)
Did each on other with deep silence look.

Th'Heroick

Th'Heroick Queen (whose high pretence to War
Cancell'd the bashful Laws and nicer Bar
Of Modesty, which did her Sex restrain)
First boldly did advance before her Train,
And thus she spake. All but a God in Name,
And that a debt Time owes unto thy Fame.

This was the first Essay of this young Lady in Poetry, but finding the Task she had undertaken hard, she laid it by till Practice and more time should make her equal to so great a Work.

To the Queen.

AS those who pass the *Alps* do say,
The Rocks which first oppose their way,
And so amazing-High do show,
By fresh Ascents appear but low,
And when they come unto the last,
They scorn the dwarfish Hills th'ave past.

So though my *Muse* at her first flight,
Thought she had chose the greatest height,
And (imp'd with *Alexander*'s Name)
Believ'd there was no further Fame:
Behold an Eye wholly Divine
Vouchsaf'd upon my Verse to Shine!
And from that time I'gan to treat
With Pitty him the World call'd *Great*;
To smile at his exalted Fate,
Unequal (though Gigantick) State.

I saw that Pitch was not sublime,
Compar'd with this which now I climb;
His Glories sunk, and were unseen,
When once appear'd the Heav'n-born Queen:
Victories, Laurels, Conquer'd Kings,
Took place among inferiour things.

Now surely I shall reach the Clouds,
For none besides such Vertue shrouds:
Having scal'd this with holy Strains,
Nought higher but the Heaven remains!
No more I'll Praise on them bestow,
Who to ill Deeds their Glories owe;
Who build their *Babels* of Renown,
Upon the poor oppressed Crown,
Whole Kingdoms do depopulate,
To raise a Proud and short-Liv'd State:
I prize no more such Frantick Might,
Than his that did with Wind-Mills Fight:
No, give me Prowess, that with Charms
Of Grace and Goodness, not with Harms,

Erects a Throne i'th' inward Parts,
And Rules mens Wills, but with their Hearts;
Who with Piety and Vertue thus
Propitiates God, and Conquers us.
O that now like *Araunah* here,
Altars of Praises I could rear,
Suiting her worth, which might be seen
Like a Queens Present, to a Queen!

'Alone she stands for Vertues Cause,
'When all decry, upholds her Laws:
'When to Banish her is the Strife,
'Keeps her unexil'd in her Life;
'Guarding her matchless Innocence
'From Storms of boldest Impudence;
'In spight of all the Scoffs and Rage,
'And Persecutions of the Age,
'Owns Vertues Altar, feeds the Flame,
'Adores her much-derided Name;
'While impiously her hands they tie,
'Loves her in her Captivity;

'Like

'Like *Perseus* saves her, when she stands
'Expos'd to the *Leviathans*.
'So did bright Lamps once live in Urns,
'So Camphire in the water burns,
'So *Ætna*'s Flames do ne'er go out,
'Though Snows do freeze her head without.

How dares bold Vice unmasked walk,
And like a Giant proudly stalk?
When Vertue's so exalted seen,
Arm'd and Triumphant in the Queen?
How dares its Ulcerous Face appear,
When Heavenly Beauty is so near?
But so when God was close at hand,
And the bright Cloud did threatning stand
(In sight of *Israel*) on the Tent,
They on in their Rebellion went.

O that I once so happy were,
To find a nearer Shelter there!
Till then poor Dove, I wandering fly
Between the Deluge and the Skie:

Till then I Mourn, but do not sing,
And oft shall plunge my wearied wing:
If her bless'd hand vouchsafe the Grace,
I'th' Ark with her to give a place,
I safe from danger shall be found,
When Vice and Folly others drown'd.

A Pastoral Dialogue.

Dorinda. Sabæan Perfumes fragrant Roses bring,
With all the Flowers that Paint the gaudy Spring:
Scatter them all in young *Alexis*'s way,
With all that's sweet and (like himself) that's Gay.

Alexis. Immortal Laurels and as lasting Praise,
Crown the Divine *Dorinda*'s matchless Laies:
May all Hearts stoop, where mine would gladly yield,
Had not *Lycoris* prepossest the Field.

Dor. Would my *Alexis* meet my noble Flame,
In all *Ausonia* neither Youth nor Dame,
Should so renown'd in Deathless Numbers shine,
As thy exalted Name should do in mine.

Alex. He'll need no Trophie nor ambitious Hearse,
Who shall be honour'd by *Dorinda*'s Verse;
But where it is inscrib'd, *That here doth lie*
Lycoris's Love. That Fame can never die.

Dor. On *Tyber*'s Bank I *Thyrsis* did espie,
And by his side did bright *Lycoris* lie;
She Crown'd his Head, and Kist his amorous Brow,
Ah Poor *Alexis!* Ah then where wer't thou?

Alex. When thou saw'st that, I ne'r had seen my Fair,
And what pass'd then ought not to be my Care;
I liv'd not then, but first began to be,
When I *Lycoris* Lov'd, and she Lov'd me.

Dor. Ah choose a Faith, a Faith that's like thine own,
A Virgin Love, a Love that's newly blown:
'Tis not enough a Maidens Heart is chast,
It must be Single, and not once mis-plac't.

Alex. Thus do our Priests of Heavenly Pastures tell,
Eternal Groves, all Earthly, that excel:

And

And think to wean us from our Loves below,
By dazling Objects which we cannot know.

On Death.

TEll me thou safest End of all our Woe,
   Why wreched Mortals do avoid thee so:
Thou gentle drier o'th' afflicteds Tears,
Thou noble ender of the Cowards Fears;
Thou sweet Repose to Lovers sad dispaire,
Thou Calm t'Ambitions rough Tempestuous Care.
If in regard of Bliss thou wert a Curse,
And then the Joys of Paradise art worse;
Yet after Man from his first Station fell,
And God from *Eden Adam* did expel,
Thou wert no more an Evil, but Relief;
The Balm and Cure to ev'ry Humane Grief:
Through thee (what Man had forfeited before),
He now enjoys, and ne'r can loose it more.

No subtile Serpents in the Grave betray,
Worms on the Body there, not Soul do prey;
No Vice there Tempts, no Terrors there afright,
No Coz'ning Sin affords a false delight:
No vain Contentions do that Peace annoy,
No feirce Alarms break the lasting Joy.

  Ah since from thee so many Blessings flow,
Such real Good as Life can never know;
Come when thou wilt, in thy afrighting'st Dress,
Thy Shape shall never make thy Welcome less.
Thou mayst to Joy, but ne'er to Fear give Birth,
Thou Best, as well as Certain'st thing on Earth.
Fly thee? May Travellers then fly their Rest,
And hungry Infants fly the profer'd Brest.
No, those that faint and tremble at thy Name,
Fly from their Good on a mistaken Fame.
Thus Childish fear did *Israel* of old
From Plenty and the Promis'd Land with-hold;
They fancy'd Giants, and refus'd to go,
When *Canaan* did with Milk and Honey flow.

First EPIGRAM.

Upon being Contented with a Little.

WE deem them moderate, but *Enough* implore,
What barely will suffice, and ask no more:
Who say, (O Jove) *a competency give*,
Neither *in Luxury, or Want we'd live.*
But what is that, which these *Enough* do call?
If both the *Indies* unto some should fall,
Such Wealth would yet *Enough* but onely be,
And what they'd term not Want, or Luxury.

    Among the Suits *O Jove,* my humbler take;
    A little give, I that Enough will make.

The Second EPIGRAM.
On BILLINDA.

WAnton *Bellinda* loudly does complain,
I've chang'd my Love of late into disdain:

Calls me unconstant, cause I now adore
The chast *Marcella*, that lov'd her before.

 Sin or Dishonour, me as well may blame,
 That I repent, or do avoid a shame.

The Third EPIGRAM.
On an ATHEIST.

*P*Osthumus boasts he does not Thunder fear,
 And for this cause would Innocent appear;
That in his Soul no Terrour he does feel,
At threatn'd Vultures, or *Ixion*'s Wheel,
Which fright the Guilty: But when *Fabius* told
What Acts 'gainst Murder lately were enrol'd,
'Gainst Incest, Rapine, ---- straight upon the Tale
His Colour chang'd, and *Posthumus* grew pale.

 His Impious Courage had no other Root,
 But that the Villaine, Atheist was to boot.

The

The Fourth EPIGRAM.
On GALLA.

Now liquid Streams by the fierce Cold do grow
As solid as the Rocks from whence they flow;
Now *Tibers* Banks with Ice united meet,
And it's firm Stream may well be term'd its Street;
Now Vot'ries 'fore the Shrines like Statues show,
And scarce the Men from Images we know;
Now Winters Palsey seizes ev'ry Age,
And none's so warm, but feels the Seasons Rage;
Even the bright Lillies and triumphant Red
Which o're *Corinna*'s youthful cheeks are spred,
Look pale and bleak, and shew a purple hew,
And Violets staine, where Roses lately grew.

Galla alone, with wonder we behold,
Maintain her Spring, and still out-brave the Cold;
Her constant white does not to Frost give place,
Nor fresh Vermillion fade upon her face:

    Sure Divine beauty in this Dame does shine?
    Not Humane, one reply'd, yet not Divine.

A Farewel
To Worldly Joys.

Farewel ye Unsubstantial Joyes,
Ye Gilded Nothings, Gaudy Toyes,
Too long ye have my Soul misled,
Too long with Aiery Diet fed:
But now my Heart ye shall no more
Deceive, as you have heretofore:
For when I hear such *Sirens* sing,
Like *Ithacas*'s fore-warned King,
With prudent Resolution I
Will so my Will and Fancy tye,
That stronger to the Mast not he,
Than I to Reason bound will be:
And though your Witchcrafts strike my Ear,
Unhurt, like him, your Charms I'll hear.

THE
Complaint of a Lover.

Seest thou younder craggy Rock,
    Whose Head o'er-looks the swelling Main,
Where never Shepherd fed his Flock,
    Or careful Peasant sow'd his Grain.

No wholesome Herb grows on the same,
    Or Bird of Day will on it rest;
'Tis Barren as the Hopeless Flame,
    That scortches my tormented Breast.

Deep underneath a Cave does lie,
    Th' entrance hid with dismal Yew,
Where *Phebus* never shew'd his Eye,
    Or cheerful Day yet pierced through.

In that dark Melancholy Cell,
  (Retreate and Sollace to my Woe)
Love, sad Dispair, and I, do dwell,
  The Springs from whence my Griefs do flow.

Treacherous Love that did appear,
  (When he at first approach't my Heart)
Drest in a Garb far from severe,
  Or threatning ought of future smart.

So Innocent those Charms then seem'd,
  When *Rosalinda* first I spy'd,
Ah! Who would them have deadly deem'd?
  But Flowrs do often Serpents hide.

Beneath those sweets conceal'd lay,
  To Love the cruel Foe, Disdain,
With which (alas) she does repay
  My Constant and Deserving Pain.

When

When I in Tears have spent the Night,
    With Sighs I usher in the Sun,
Who never saw a sadder sight,
    In all the Courses he has run.

Sleep, which to others Ease does prove,
    Comes unto me, alas, in vain:
For in my Dreams I am in Love,
    And in them too she does Disdain.

Some times t'Amuse my Sorrow, I
    Unto the hollow Rocks repair,
And loudly to the *Eccho* cry,
    Ah! gentle Nimph come ease my Care.

Thou who, times past, a Lover wer't,
    Ah! pity me, who now am so,
And by a sense of thine own smart,
    Alleviate my Mighty Woe.

Come Flatter then, or Chide my Grief;
    Catch my laſt Words, and call me Fool;
Or ſay, ſhe Loves, for my Relief;
    My Paſſion either ſooth, or School.

Love, the Soul of Poetry.

When firſt *Alexis* did in Verſe delight,
    His Muſe in Low, but Graceful Numbers walk't,
And now and then a little Proudly ſtalk't;
    But never aim'd at any noble Flight:
The Herds, the Groves, the gentle purling Streams,
Adorn'd his Song, and were his higheſt Theams.

But Love theſe Thoughts, like Miſts, did ſoon diſperſe,
Enlarg'd his Fancy, and ſet free his Muſe,
Biding him more Illuſtrious Subjects chooſe;
    The Acts of Gods, and God-like Men reherſe.
From thence new Raptures did his Breaſt inſpire,
His ſcarce Warm-Heart converted was to Fire.

Th'

Th' exalted Poet rais'd by this new Flame,
With Vigor flys, where late he crept along,
And Acts Divine, in a Diviner Song,
  Commits to the eternal Trompe of Fame.
And thus *Alexis* does prove Love to be,
As the Worlds Soul, the Soul of Poetry.

To my Lady Berkeley,

Afflicted upon her Son, My Lord BERKELEY's Early Engaging in the Sea-Service.

SO the renown'd *Ithacasian* Queen
In Tears for her *Telemachus* was seen,
When leaving Home, he did attempt the Ire
Of rageing Seas, to seek his absent Sire:
Such bitter Sighs her tender Breast did rend;
But had she known a God did him attend,
And would with Glory bring him safe again,
Bright Thoughts would then have dispossess't her Pain.

Ah Noblest Lady! You that her excel
In every Vertue, may in Prudence well
Suspend your Care; knowing what power befriends
Your Hopes, and what on Vertue still attends.

In bloody Conflicts he will Armour find,
In strongest Tempests he will rule the Wind,
He will through Thousand Dangers force a way,
And still Triumphant will his Charge convey.
And the All-ruling power that can act thus,
Will safe return your Dear *Telemachus*.

  Alas, he was not born to live in Peace,
Souls of his Temper were not made for Ease,
Th'Ignoble only live secure from Harms,
The Generous tempt, and seek out fierce Alarms.
Huge Labours were for *Hercules* design'd,
Jason, to fetch the Golden Fleece, enjoyn'd,
The *Minotaure* by Noble *Theseus* dy'd,
In vain were Valour, if it were not try'd,
Should the admir'd and far-sought Diamond lye,
As in its Bed, unpolisht to the Eye,
It would be slighted like a common stone,
It's Value would be small, its Glory none.
But when't has pass'd the Wheel and Cutters hand,
Then it is meet in Monarchs Crowns to stand.

Upon the Noble Object of your Care
Heaven has bestow'd, of Worth, so large a share,
That unastonisht none can him behold,
Or credit all the Wonders of him told!
When others, at his Years were turning o're,
The Acts of Heroes that had liv'd before,
Their Valour to excite, when time should fit,
He then did Things, were Worthy to be writ!
Stayd not for Time, his Courage that out-ran
In Actions, far before in Years, a Man.
Two *French* Campagnes he boldly courted Fame,
While his Face more the Maid, than Youth became
Adde then to these a Soul so truly Mild,
Though more than Man, Obedient as a Child.
And (ah) should one Small Isle all these confine,
Vertues created through the World to shine?
Heaven that forbids, and Madam so should you;
Remember he but bravely does pursue
His Noble Fathers steps; with your own Hand
Then Gird his Armour on, like him he'll stand,
His Countries Champion, and Worthy be
Of your High Vertue, and his Memory.

St.

[27]

St. John Baptist *Painted by her self in the Wilderness, with Angels appearing to him, and with a Lamb by him.*

THe Sun's my Fire, when it does shine,
The hollow Spring's my Cave of Wine,
The Rocks and Woods afford me Meat;
This Lamb and I on one Dish eat:
The neighbouring Herds my Garments send,
My Pallet the kind Earth doth lend:
Excess and Grandure I decline,
M'Associates onely are Divine.

HERODIAS *Daughter presenting to her Mother St.* JOHN's *Head in a Charger, also Painted by her self.*

Behold, dear Mother, who was late our Fear,
Disarm'd and Harmless, I present you here;
The Tongue ty'd up, that made all *Jury* quake,
And which so often did our Greatness shake;

No Terror sits upon his Awful Brow,

Where Fierceness reign'd, there Calmness triumphs now;

As Lovers use, he gazes on my Face,

With Eyes that languish, as they sued for Grace;

Wholly subdu'd by my Victorious Charms,

See how his Head reposes in my Arms.

Come, joyn then with me in my just Transport,

Who thus have brought the Hermite to the Court.

On a Picture Painted by her self, representing two Nimphs of DIANA's, *one in a posture to Hunt, the other Batheing.*

WE are *Diana*'s Virgin-Train,
    Descended of no Mortal Strain;
Our Bows and Arrows are our Goods,
Our Pallaces, the lofty Woods,
The Hills and Dales, at early Morn,
Resound and Eccho with our Horn;
We chase the Hinde and Fallow-Deer,
The Wolf and Boar both dread our Spear;

[29]

In Swiftness we out-strip the Wind,
An Eye and Thought we leave behind;
We *Fawns* and Shaggy *Satyrs* awe;
To *Sylvan Pow'rs* we give the Law:
Whatever does provoke our Hate,
Our Javelins strike, as sure as *Fate*;
We Bathe in Springs, to cleanse the Soil,
Contracted by our eager Toil;
~~In which we shine like glittering Beams,~~
~~Or Christal in the Christal Streams;~~
Though *Venus* we transcend in Form,
No wanton Flames our Bosomes warm!
If you ask where such Wights do dwell,
In what Bless't Clime, that so excel?
The Poets onely that can tell.

An Invective against Gold.

OF all the Poisons that the fruitful Earth
E'er yet brought forth, or Monsters she gave Birth,
Nought to Mankind has e'er so fatal been,
As thou, accursed Gold, their Care and Sin.

Methinks I the Advent'rous Merchant see,
Ploughing the faithless Seas, in search of thee,
His dearest Wife and Children left behind,
(His real Wealth) while he, a Slave to th' Wind,
Sometimes becalm'd, the Shore with longing Eyes
Wishes to see, and what he wishes, Spies:
For a rude Tempest wakes him from his Dream,
And Strands his Bark by a more sad Extream.
Thus, hopless Wretch, is his whole Life-time spent,
And though thrice Wreck't, 's no Wiser than he went.

Again, I see, the Heavenly Fair despis'd,
A Hagg like Hell, with Gold, more highly priz'd;
Mens Faith betray'd, their Prince and Country Sold,
Their God deny'd, all for the Idol Gold.

Unhappy Wretch, who first found out the Oar,
What kind of Vengeance rests for thee in store?
If *Nebats* Son, that *Israel* led astray,
Meet a severe Reward at the last Day?
Some strange unheard-of Judgement thou wilt find,
Who thus hast caus'd to Sin all Humane Kind.

The Miseries of Man.

IN that so temperate Soil *Arcadia* nam'd,
For fertile Pasturage by Poets fam'd;
Stands a steep Hill, whose lofty jetting Crown,
Casts o'er the neighbouring Plains, a seeming Frown;
Close at its mossie Foot an aged Wood,
Compos'd of various Trees, there long has stood,
Whose thick united Tops scorn the Sun's Ray,
And hardly will admit the Eye of Day.
By oblique windings through this gloomy Shade,
Has a clear purling Stream its Passage made,
The *Nimph*, as discontented seem'd t'ave chose
This sad Recess to murmur forth her Woes.

To this Retreat, urg'd by tormenting Care,
The melancholly *Cloris* did repair,

As a fit Place to take the sad Relief
Of Sighs and Tears, to ease oppressing Grief.
Near to the Mourning *Nimph* she chose a Seat,
And these Complaints did to the Shades repeat.

Ah wretched, truly wretched Humane Race!
Your Woes from what Beginning shall I trace,
Where End, from your first feeble New-born Cryes,
To the last Tears that wet your dying Eyes?
Man, Common Foe, assail'd on ev'ry hand,
Finds that no Ill does Neuter by him stand,
Inexorable Death, Lean Poverty,
Pale Sickness, ever sad Captivity.
Can I, alas, the sev'ral Parties name,
Which, muster'd up, the Dreadful Army frame?
And sometimes in One Body all Unite,
Sometimes again do separately fight:
While sure Success on either Way does waite,
Either a Swift, or else a Ling'ring Fate.

But why 'gainst thee, O *Death!* should I inveigh,
That to our Quiet art the only way?

And yet I would (could I thy Dart command)
Crie, Here O strike! and there O hold thy Hand!
The Lov'd, the Happy, and the Youthful spare,
And end the Sad, the Sick, the Poor Mans Care.
But whether thou or Blind, or Cruel art,
Whether 'tis Chance, or Malice, guides thy Dart,
Thou from the Parents Arms dost pull away
The hopeful Child, their Ages only stay:
The Two, whom Friendship in dear Bands has ty'd,
Thou dost with a remorseless hand devide;
Friendship, the Cement, that does faster twine
Two Souls, than that which Soul and Body joyn:
Thousands have been, who their own Blood did spill,
But never any yet his Friend did kill.
Then 'gainst thy Dart what Armour can be found,
Who, where thou do'st not strike, do'st deepest wound?
Thy Pitty, than thy Wrath's more bitter far,
Most cruel, where 'twould seem the most to spare:
Yet thou of many Evils art but One,
Though thou by much too many art alone.

What

What shall I say of *Poverty*, whence flows?
To miserable Man so many Woes?
Rediculous Evil which too oft we prove,
Does Laughter cause, where it should Pitty move;
Solitary Ill, into which no Eye,
Though ne're so Curious, ever cares to pry,
And were there, 'mong such plenty, onely One
Poor Man, he certainly would live alone.

Yet *Poverty* does leave the Man entire,
But *Sickness* nearer Mischiefs does conspire;
Invades the Body with a loath'd Embrace,
Prides both its Strength, and Beauty to deface;
Nor does its Malice in these bounds restrain,
But shakes the Throne of Sacred Wit, the Brain,
And with a ne're enough detested Force
Reason disturbs, and turns out of its Course.
Again, when Nature some Rare Piece has made,
On which her Utmost Skill she seems t'ave laid,
Polish't, adorn'd the Work with moving Grace,
And in the Beauteous Frame a Soul doth place,

So perfectly compos'd, it makes Divine
Each Motion, Word, and Look from thence does shine;
This Goodly Composition, the Delight
Of ev'ry Heart, and Joy of ev'ry sight,
Its peevish Malice has the Power to spoyle,
And with a Sully'd Hand its Lusture soyle.
The Grief were Endless, that should all bewaile,
Against whose sweet Repose thou dost prevail:
Some freeze with Agues, some with Feavers burn,
Whose Lives thou half out of their Holds dost turn;
And of whose Sufferings it may be said,
They living feel the very State o'th' Dead.
Thou in a thousand sev'ral Forms are drest,
And in them all dost Wretched Man infest.

And yet as if these Evils were too few,
Men their own Kind with hostile Arms pursue;
Not Heavens fierce Wrath, nor yet the Hate of Hell,
Not any Plague that e're the World befel,
Not Inundations, Famines, Fires blind rage,
Did ever Mortals equally engage,

As

As Man does Man, more skilful to annoy,
Both Mischievous and Witty to destroy.
The bloody Wolf, the Wolf does not pursue;
The Boar, though fierce, his Tusk will not embrue
In his own Kind, Bares, not on Bares do prey:
Then art thou, Man, more savage far than they.

And now, methinks, I present do behold
The Bloudy Fields that are in Fame enroll'd,
I see, I see thousands in Battle slain,
The Dead and Dying cover all the Plain,.
Confused Noises hear, each way sent out,
The Vanquishts Cries joyn'd with the Victors shout;
Their Sighs and Groans who draw a painful Breath,
And feel the Pangs of slow approaching Death:
Yet happier these, far happier are the Dead;.
Than who into Captivity are led:
What by their Chains, and by the Victors Pride,
We pity these, and envy those that dy'd:
And who can say, when Thousands are betray'd,
To Widdowhood, Orphants or Childless made.

Whither the Day does draw more Tears or Blood
A greater Chryſtal, or a Crimſon Floud.
The faithful Wife, who late her Lord did Arm,
And hop'd to ſhield, by holy Vows, from Harm,
Follow'd his parting-ſteps with Love and Care,
Sent after weeping Eyes, while he afar
Rod heated on, born by a brave Diſdain,
May now go ſeek him, lying 'mong the Slain:
Low on the Earth ſhe'l find his lofty Creſt,
And thoſe refulgent Arms which late his Breaſt
Did guard, by rough Encounters broke and tore,
His Face and Hair, with Brains all clotted ore,
And Warlike Weeds beſmeer'd with Duſt and Gore.

And will the Suffering World never beſtow
Upon th'Accurſed Cauſers of ſuch Woe,
A vengeance that may parallel their Loſs,
Fix Publick Thieves and Robbers on the Croſs?
Such as call Ruine, Conqueſt, in their Pride,
And having plagu'd Mankind, in Triumph ride.
Like that renounced Murderer who ſtaines
In theſe our days *Alſatias* fertile Plains,

Only

Only to fill the future Tromp of Fame,
Though greater Crimes, than Glory it proclame.
Alcides, Scourge of Thieves, return to Earth,
Which uncontrolled gives such Monsters birth;
On *Scepter'd-Cacus* let thy Power be shown,
Pull him not from his Den, but from his Throne.

Clouds of black Thoughts her further Speech here broke,
Her swelling Grief too great was to be spoke,
Which strugl'd long in her tormented Mind,
Till it some Vent by Sighs and Tears did find.
And when her Sorrow something was subdu'd,
She thus again her sad Complaint renewed.

Most Wretched Man, were th'Ills I nam'd before
All which I could in thy sad State deplore,
Did Things without alone 'gainst thee prevail,
My Tongue I'de chide, that them I did bewaile:
But, Shame to Reason, thou art seen to be
Unto thy self the fatall'st Enemy,
Within thy Breast the Greatest Plagues to bear,
First them to breed; and then to cherish there;

Unmanag'd Passions which the Reins have broke
Of Reason, and refuse to bear its Yoke.
But hurry thee, uncurb'd, from place to place,
A wild, unruly, and an Uncouth Chace.
Now cursed Gold does lead the Man astray,
False flatt'ring Honours do anon betray,
Then Beauty does as dang'roufly delude,
Beauty, that vanishes, while 'tis pursu'd,
That, while we do behold it, fades away,
And even a Long Encomium will not stay.

Each one of these can the Whole Man employ,
Nor knows he anger, sorrow, fear, or joy,
But what to these relate; no Thought does start
Aside, but tends to its appointed Part,
No Respite to himself from Cares he gives,
But on the Rack of Expectation lives.
If crost, the Torment cannot be exprest,
Which boyles within his agitated Breast.
Musick is harsh, all Mirth is an offence,
The Choicest Meats cannot delight his Sense,

Hard

Hard as the Earth he feels his Downy Bed,
His Pillow stufft with Thornes, that bears his Head,
He rolls from side to side, in vain seeks Rest;
For if sleep comes at last to the Distrest,
His Troubles then cease not to vex him too,
But Dreams present, what he does waking do.
On th'other side, if he obtains the Prey,
And Fate to his impetuous Sute gives way,
Be he or Rich, or Amorous, or Great,
He'll find this Riddle still of a Defeat,
That only Care, for Bliss, he home has brought,
Or else Contempt of what he so much sought;
So that on each Event if we reflect,
The Joys and Sufferings of both sides collect,
We cannot say where lies the greatest Pain,
In the fond Pursuit, Loss, or Empty Gain.

And can it be, Lord of the Sea and Earth,
Off-spring of Heaven, that to thy State and Birth
Things so incompatible should be joyn'd,
Passions should thee confound, to Heaven assign'd?

Passions that do the Soul unguarded lay,
And to the strokes of Fortune ope' a way.
Were't not that these thy Force did from thee take,
How bold, how brave Resistance would'st thou make?
Defie the Strength and Malice of thy Foes,
Unmoved stand the Worlds United Blows?
For what is't, Man, unto thy Better Part,
That thou or Sick, or Poor, or Captive art?
Since no Material Stroke the Soul can feel,
The smart of Fire, or yet the Edge of Steel.
As little can it Worldly Joys partake,
Though it the Body does its Agent make,
And joyntly with it Servile Labour bear,
For Things, alas, in which it cannot share.
Surveigh the Land and Sea by Heavens embrac't,
Thou'lt find no sweet th'Immortal Soul can tast:
Why dost thou then, O Man! thy self torment
Good here to gain; or Evils to prevent?
Who only Miserable or Happy art,
As thou neglects, or wisely act'st thy Part.

For shame then rouse thy self as from a Sleep,
The long neglected Reins let Reason keep,

The

The Charret mount, and use both Lash and Bit,
Nobly resolve, and thou wilt firmly sit:
Fierce Anger, boggling Fear, Pride prauncing still,
Bounds-hating Hope, Desire which nought can fill,
Are stubborn all, but thou may'st give them Law;
Th'are hard-Mouth'd Horses, but they well can draw.
Lash on, and the well govern'd Charret drive,
Till thou a Victor at the Goal arrive,
Where the free Soul does all her burden leave,
And Joys commensurate to her self receive.

Upon the saying that my VERSES *were made by another.*

NExt Heaven my Vows to thee (O Sacred *Muse!*)
I offer'd up, nor didst thou them refuse.

O Queen of Verse, said I, if thou'lt inspire,
And warm my Soul with thy Poetique Fire,
No Love of Gold shall share with thee my Heart,
Or yet Ambition in my Brest have Part,
More Rich, more Noble I will ever hold
The *Muses* Laurel, than a Crown of Gold.
An Undivided Sacrifice I'le lay
Upon thine Altar, Soul and Body pay;
Thou shalt my Pleasure, my Employment be,
My All I'le make a Holocaust to thee.

The Deity that ever does attend
Prayers so sincere, to mine did condescend.
I writ, and the Judicious prais'd my Pen:
Could any doubt Insuing Glory then?

What

What pleasing Raptures fill'd my Ravisht Sense?
How strong, how Sweet, Fame, was thy Influence?
And thine, False Hope, that to my flatter'd sight
Didst Glories represent so Near, and Bright?
By thee deceiv'd, methought, each Verdant Tree,
Apollos transform'd *Daphne* seem'd to be;
And ev'ry fresher Branch, and ev'ry Bow
Appear'd as Garlands to empale my Brow.
The Learn'd in Love say, Thus the Winged Boy
Does first approach, drest up in welcome Joy;
At first he to the Cheated Lovers sight
Nought represents, but Rapture and Delight,
Alluring Hopes, Soft Fears, which stronger bind
Their Hearts, than when they more assurance find.

Embolden'd thus, to Fame I did commit,
(By some few hands) my most Unlucky Wit.
But, ah, the sad effects that from it came!
What ought t'have brought me Honour, brought me shame!
Like *Esops* Painted Jay I seem'd to all,
Adorn'd in Plumes, I not my own could call:

Rifl'd

Rifl'd like her, each one my Feathers tore,
And, as they thought, unto the Owner bore.
My Laurels thus an Others Brow adorn'd,
My Numbers they Admir'd, but Me they scorn'd:
An others Brow, that had so rich a store
Of Sacred Wreaths, that circled it before;
Where mine quite lost, (like a small stream that ran
Into a Vast and Boundless Ocean)
Was swallow'd up, with what it joyn'd and drown'd,
And that Abiss yet no Accession found.

Orinda, (*Albions* and her Sexes Grace)
Ow'd not her Glory to a Beauteous Face,
It was her Radiant Soul that shon With-in,
Which struk a Lustre through her Outward Skin;
That did her Lips and Cheeks with Roses dy,
Advanc't her Height, and Sparkled in her Eye.
Nor did her Sex at all obstruct her Fame,
But higher 'mong the Stars it fixt her Name;
What she did write, not only all allow'd,
But ev'ry Laurel, to her Laurel, bow'd!

Th'Envious

Th'Envious Age, only to Me alone,
Will not allow, what I do write, my Own,
But let 'em Rage, and 'gainst a Maide Conspire,
So Deathless Numbers from my Tuneful Lyre
Do ever flow ; so *Phebus* I by thee
Divinely Inspired and possest may be ;
I willingly accept *Cassandras* Fate,
To speak the Truth, although believ'd too late.

On the Birth-Day of
Queen Katherine.

While yet it was the Empire of the Night,
    And Stars still check'r'd Darkness with their Light,
From Temples round the cheerful Bells did ring,
But with the Peales a churlish Storm did sing.
I slumbr'd ; and the Heavens like things did show,
Like things which I had seen and heard below.
Playing on Harps Angels did singing fly,
But through a cloudy and a troubl'd Sky,

Some fixt a Throne, and Royal Robes display'd,
And then a Massie Cross upon it laid.
I wept: and earnestly implor'd to know,
Why Royal Ensigns were disposed so.
An Angel said, The Emblem thou hast seen,
Denotes the Birth-Day of a Saint and Queen.
Ah, Glorious Minister, I then reply'd,
Goodness and Bliss together do reside
In Heaven and thee, why then on Earth below
These two combin'd so rarely do we know?
He said, Heaven so decrees: and such a Sable Morne
Was that, in which the *Son of God* was borne.
Then Mortal wipe thine Eyes, and cease to rave,
God darkn'd Heaven, when He the World did save.

TO
My Lord Colrane,

In Answer to his Complemental Verses sent me under the Name of CLEANOR.

Long my dull *Muse* in heavy slumbers lay,
Indulging Sloth, and to soft Ease gave way,
Her Fill of Rest resolving to enjoy,
Or fancying little worthy her employ.
When Noble *Cleanors* obliging Strains
Her, the neglected Lyre to tune, constrains.
Confus'd at first, she rais'd her drowsie Head,
Ponder'd a while, then pleas'd, forsook her Bed.
Survey'd each Line with Fancy richly fraught,
Re-read, and then revolv'd them in her Thought.

And can it be? she said, and can it be?
That 'mong the Great Ones I a Poet see?

The Great Ones? who their Ill-spent time devide,
'Twixt dang'rous Politicks, and formal Pride,
Destructive Vice, expensive Vanity,
In worse Ways yet, if Worse there any be:
Leave to Inferiours the despised Arts,
Let their Retainers be the *Men of Parts*.
But here with Wonder and with Joy I find,
I'th' Noble Born, a no less Noble Mind;
One, who on Ancestors, does not rely
For Fame, in Merit, as in Title, high!

The Severe Godess thus approv'd the Laies:
Yet too much pleas'd, alas, with her own Praise.
But to vain Pride, *My Muse*, cease to give place,
Virgils immortal Numbers once did grace
A *Smother'd Gnat*: by high Applause is shown,
If undeserv'd, the Praisers worth alone:
Nor that you should believ't, is't always meant,
'Tis often for Instruction only sent,
To praise men to Amendment, and display,
By its Perfection, where their Weakness lay.
This Use of these Applauding Numbers make
Them for Example, not Encomium, take.

The

The Discontent.

I.

Ere take no Care, take here no Care, my *Muse*,
  Nor ought of Art or Labour use:
But let thy Lines rude and unpolisht go,
Nor Equal be their Feet, nor Num'rous let them flow.
The ruggeder my Measures run when read,
They'l livelier paint th'unequal Paths fond Mortals tread.
  Who when th'are tempted by the smooth Ascents,
    Which flatt'ring Hope presents,
  Briskly they clime, and Great Things undertake;
  But Fatal Voyages, alas, they make:
    For 'tis not long before their Feet,
    Inextricable Mazes meet,
    Perplexing Doubts obstruct their Way,
    Mountains with-stand them of Dismay;
  Or to the Brink of black Dispaire them lead,
    Where's nought their Ruine to impede,

In vain for Aide they then to Reason call,
Their Senses dazle, and their Heads turn round,
The sight does all their Pow'rs confound,
And headlong down the horrid Precipice they fall:
Where storms of Sighs for ever blow,
Where raped streams of Tears do flow,
Which drown them in a Briny Floud.
My Muse pronounce aloud, there's nothing Good,
Nought that the World can show,
Nought that it can bestow.

II.

Not boundless Heaps of its admired Clay,
Ah, too successful to betray,
When spread in our fraile Vertues way:
For few do run with so Resolv'd a Pace,
That for the Golden Apple will not loose the Race.
And yet not all the Gold the Vain would spend,
Or greedy Avarice would wish to save;
Which on the Earth refulgent Beams doth send,
Or in the Sea has found a Grave,
Joyn'd in one Mass, can Bribe sufficient be,
The Body from a stern Disease to free,

Or purchase for the Minds relief
One Moments sweet Repose, when restless made by grief,
But what may Laughter, more than Pity, move:
   When some the Price of what they Dear'st Love
   Are Masters of, and hold it in their Hand,
   To part with it their Hearts they can't command:
   But chose to miss, what miss't does them torment;
   And that to hug, affords them no Content.
   Wise Fools, to do them Right, we these must hold,
   Who Love depose, and Homage pay to Gold.

III.
Nor yet, if rightly understood,
   Does Grandeur carry more of Good;
To be o'th' Number of the Great enroll'd,
A Scepter o're a Mighty Realm to hold.
      For what is this?
      If I not judge amiss.
But all th'Afflicted of a Land to take,
And of one single Family to make?
   The Wrong'd, the Poor, th'Opprest, the Sad,
   The Ruin'd, Malecontent, and Mad?

                              Which

Which a great Part of ev'ry Empire frame,
And Interest in the common Father claime.
Again what is't, but always to abide
A Gazing Crowd ? upon a Stage to spend
A Life that's vain, or Evil without End?
And which is yet nor safely held, nor laid aside ?
And then, if lesser Titles carry less of Care,
Yet none but Fools ambitious are to share
Such a Mock-Good, of which 'tis said, 'tis Best,
When of the least of it Men are possest.

IV.
But, O, the Laurel'd Fool! that doats on Fame,
Whose Hope's Applause, whose Fear's to want a Name;
  Who can accept for Pay
  Of what he does, what others say ;
Exposes now to hostile Arms his Breast,
To toylsome Study then betrays his Rest ;
Now to his Soul denies a just Content,
Then forces on it what it does resent ;
And all for Praise of Fools : for such are those,
Which most of the Admiring Crowd compose.
O famisht Soul, which such Thin Food can feed !
O Wretched Labour crown'd with such a Meed!   Too

Too loud, O Fame! thy Trumpet is, too shrill,
    To lull a Mind to Rest,
    Or calme a stormy Breast,
  Which asks a Musick soft and still.
  'Twas not *Amaleck*'s vanquisht Cry,
  Nor *Israels* shout of Victory,
  That could in *Saul* the rising Passion lay,
'Twas the soft strains of *David*'s Lyre the Evil Spirit chace't away.

V.

But Friendship fain would yet it self defend,
    And Mighty Things it does pretend,
  To be of this Sad Journey, Life, the Baite;
The sweet Refection of our toylsome State.
  But though True Friendship a Rich Cordial be,
    Alas, by most 'tis so alay'd,
    Its Good so mixt with Ill we see,
    That Dross for Gold is often paid.
  And for one Grain of Friendship that is found,
  Falshood and Interest do the Mass compound,
Or coldness, worse than Steel, the Loyal heart doth wound.
  Love in no Two was ever yet the same,
  No Happy Two ere felt an Equal Flame.

VI.

Is there that Earth by Humane Foot ne're preſt?
That Aire which never yet by Humane Breaſt
Reſpir'd, did Life ſupply?

    Oh, thither let me fly!

    Where from the World at ſuch a diſtance ſet,
All that's paſt, preſent, and to come I may forget:
    The Lovers Sighs, and the Afflicteds Tears,
    What e're may wound my Eyes or Ears.

    The grating Noiſe of Private Jars,
    The horrid ſound of Publick Wars,
    Of babling Fame the Idle Stories,
    The ſhort-liv'd Triumphs Noyſy-Glories,
    The Curious Nets the ſubtile weave,
    The Word, the Look that may deceive.
No Mundan Care ſhall more affect my Breaſt,
    My profound Peace ſhake or moleſt:
But *Stupor*, like to Death, my Senſes bind,
    That ſo I may anticipate that Reſt,
Which only in my Grave I hope to find.

A

A Pastoral Dialogue.

Amintor. Stay gentle Nymph, nor so solic'tous be?
To fly his sight that still would gaze on thee.
With other Swaines I see thee oft converse,
Content to speak, and hear what they rehearse:
But I unhappy, when I e're draw nigh,
Thou streight do'st leave both Place, and Company.
If this thy Flight, from fear of Harm doth flow,
Ah, sure thou little of my Heart dost know.

Alinda. What wonder, Swain, if the Pursu'd by Flight,
Seeks to avoid the close Pursuers Sight?
And if no Cause I have to fly from thee,
Then thou hast none, why thou dost follow me.

Amin. If to the Cause thou wilt propitious prove,
Take it at once, fair Nymph, and know 'tis Love.

Alinda.

Alin. To my just Pray'r, ye favouring Gods attend,
These Vows to Heaven with equal Zeal I send,
My flocks from Wolves, my Heart from Love, defend.

Amin. The Gods which did on thee such Charms bestow,
Ne're meant thou shouldst to Love have prov'd a Foe,
That so Divine a Power thou shouldst defy.
Could there a Reason be, I'd ask thee, why?

Alin. Why does *Licoris*, once so bright and gay,
Pale as a Lilly pine her self away?
Why does *Elvira*, ever sad, frequent
The lonely shades? Why does yon Monument
Which we upon our Left Hand do behold,
Hapless *Amintas* youthful Limbs enfold?
Say Shepherd, say: But if thou wilt not tell,
Damon, *Philisides*, and *Strephon* well
Can speak the Cause, whose Falshood each upbraids,
And justly me from Cruel Love disswades.

Amin. Hear me ye Gods. Me and my Flocks forsake,
If e're like them my promis'd Faith I brake.

Alinda.

Alin. By others sad Experience wise I'le be,

Amin. But such thy Wisdom highly injures me:
And nought but Death can give a Remedy.
Ye Learn'd in Physick, what does it avail,
That you by Art (wherein ye never fail)
Present Relief have for the Mad-dogs Bite?
The Serpents sting? the poisonous *Achonite?*
While helpless Love upbraids your baffl'd skill,
And far more certain, than the rest, doth kill.

Alin. Fond Swain, go dote upon the new blown Rose,
Whose Beauty with the Morning did disclose,
And e're Days King forsakes th'enlighted Earth,
Wither'd, returns from whence it took its Birth.
As much Excuse will there thy Love attend,
As what thou dost on Womens Beauty spend.

Amin. Ah Nymph, those Charms which I in thee admire,
Can, nor before, nor with thy Life expire.
From Heaven they are, and such as ne're can dye,
But with thy Soul they will ascend the Sky!
For though my ravisht Eye beholds in Thee,
Such beauty as I can in none else see;

That Nature there alone is without blame,
Yet did not this my faithful Heart enflame:
Nor when in Dance thou mov'st upon the Plaine,
Or other Sports pursu'st among the Train
Of choicest Nymphs, where thy attractive Grace
Shews thee alone, though thousands be in place!
Yet not for these do I *Alinda* love,
Hear then what 'tis, that does my Passion move.

That Thou still Earliest at the Temple art,
And still the last that does from thence depart;
Pans Altar is by thee the oftnest prest,
Thine's still the fairest Offering and the Best;
And all thy other Actions seem to be,
The true Result of Unfeign'd Piety;
Strict in thy self, to others Just and Mild;
Careful, nor to Deceive, nor be Beguil'd;
Wary, without the least Offence, to live,
Yet none than thee more ready to forgive!
Even on thy Beauty thou dost Fetters lay,
Leaft, unawares, it any should betray.
Far unlike, sure, to many of thy Sex,
Whose Pride it is, the doting World to vex;

Spreading

Spreading their Universal Nets to take
Who e're their artifice can captive make.
But thou command'st thy Sweet, but Modest Eye,
That no Inviting Glance from thence should fly.
Beholding with a Gen'rous Disdain,
The lighter Courtships of each amorous Swain;
Knowing, true Fame, Vertue alone can give:
Nor dost thou greedily even that receive.
And what 'bove this thy Character can raise?
Thirsty of Merit, yet neglecting Praise!
While daily these Perfections I discry,
Matchless *Alinda* makes me daily dy.
Thou absent, Flow'rs to me no Odours yield,
Nor find I freshness in the dewy Field;
Not *Thyrsis* Voice, nor *Melibeus* Lire,
Can my Sad Heart with one Gay Thought inspire;
My thriving Flock ('mong Shepherds Vows the Chief)
I unconcern'd behold, as they my Grief.

This I profess, if this thou not believe,
A further proof I ready am to give,
Command: there's nothing I'le not undertake,
And, thy Injunctions, Love will easie make.

Ah,

Ah, if thou could'st incline a gentle Ear,
Of plighted Faith, and hated *Hymen* hear;
Thou hourly then my spotless Love should'st see,
That all my Study, how to please, should be;
How to protect thee from disturbing Care,
And in thy Griefs to bear the greatest share;
Nor should a Joy, my Warie Heart surprize,
That first I read not in thy charming Eyes.

Alin. If ever I to any do impart,
My, till this present hour, well-guarded Heart,
That Passion I have fear'd, I'le surely prove,
For one that does, like to *Amintor* love.

Amintor. Ye Gods------

Alin. Shepherd, no more: enough it is that I,
Thus long to Love, have listn'd patiently.
Farewel: *Pan* keep thee, Swain.

Amintor. And Blessings Thee,
Rare as thy Vertues, still accompany.

A

A Pastoral Dialogue

Melibæus, Alcippe, Asteria, Licida, Alcimedon, *and* Amira.

Melibæus. Welcome fair Nymphs, most welcome to this shade,
Distemp'ring Heats do now the Plains invade:
But you may sit, from Sun securely here,
If you an old mans company not fear.

Alcippe. Most Reverend Swaine, far from us ever be
The imputation of such Vanity.
From Hill to Holt w'ave thee unweary'd sought,
And bless the Chance that us hath hither brought.

Asteria. Fam'd *Melibæus* for thy Virtuous Lays,
If thou dost not disdain our Female Praise,
We come to sue thou would'st to us recite
One of thy Songs, which gives such high delight
To ev'ry Eare, wherein thou dost dispense
Sage Precepts cloath'd in flowing Eloquence.

Licida.

Licida. Fresh Garlands we will make for thee each morne,
Thy reverend Head to shade, and to adorne;
To cooling Springs thy fainting Flock we'll guide,
All thou command'st, to do shall be our Pride.

Meli. Cease, gentle Nymphs, the Willing to entreat,
To have your Wish, each needs but take a Seat.
With joy I shall my ancient Art revive,
With which, when Young, I did for Glory strive.
Nor for my Verse will I accept a Hire,
Your bare Attentions all I shall require.

Alci. Lo, from the Plain I see draw near a Pair
That I could wish in our Converse might share.
Amira 'tis and young *Alcimedon*.

Lici. Serious Discourse industriously they shun.

Alci. It being yet their luck to come this way,
The Fond Ones to our Lecture we'll betray:
And though they only sought a private shade,
Perhaps they may depart more Vertuous made.

I will accost them. Gentle Nymph and Swaine,
Good *Melibæus* us doth entertain
With Lays Divine: if you'll his Hearers be,
Take streight your Seats without Apology.

Alcimedon.

Alci. Paying short thanks, at fair *Amiras* feet,
I'le lay me down: let her choose where 'tis meet.

Al. Shepherd, behold, we all attentive sit.

Meli. What shall I sing? what shall my *Muse* reherse?
Love is a Theme well sutes a Past'ral Verse,
That gen'ral Error, Universal Ill,
That Darling of our Weakness and our Will;
By which though many fall, few hold it shame;
Smile at the Fault, which they would seem to blame.
What wonder then, if those with Mischief play,
It to destruction them doth oft betray?

But by experience it is daily found,
That Love the softer Sex does sorest wound;
In Mind, as well as Body, far more weak
Than Men: therefore to them my Song shall speak,
Advising well, however it succeed:
But unto All I say, *Of Love take heed.*
So hazardous, because so hard to know
On whom they are we do our Hearts bestow;
How they will use them, or with what regard
Our Faith and high Esteem they will reward:

K

For

For few are found, that truly acted be
By Principles of Generosity.
That when they know a Virgins Heart they've gain'd,
(And though by many Vows and Arts obtain'd)
Will think themselves oblig'd their Faith to hold
Tempted by Friends, by Interest, or by Gold.
Expect it not: most, Love their Pastime make,
Lightly they Like, and lightly they forsake ;
Their Roving Humour wants but a pretence
With Oaths and what's most Sacred to dispence.

When unto such a Maid has given her Heart,
And said, *Alone my Happiness thou art,*
In thee and in thy Truth I place my Rest.
Her sad Surprize how can it be exprest,
When all on which she built her Joy she finds,
Vanish, like Clouds, disperst before the Winds ;
Her self, who th'adored Idol wont to be,
A poor despis'd Idolater to see ?
Regardless Tears she may profusely spend,
Unpitty'd sighs her tender Breast may rend :
But the false Image she will ne're erace,
Though far unworthy still to hold its place :

So

So hard it is, even Wiser grown, to take
Th'Impression out, which Fancy once did make.
Believe me Nymphs, believe my hoary hairs,
Truth and Experience waits on many years.

Before the Eldest of you Light beheld,
A Nymph we had, in Beauty all excell'd,
Rodanthe call'd, in whom each Grace did shine,
Could make a Mortal Maid appear Divine.
And none could say, where most her Charms did lye,
In her inchanting Tongue, or conquering Eye.
Her Vertue yet her Beauties so out-shon,
As Beauty did the Garments she put on!

Among the Swains, which here their Flocks then fed,
Alcander with the highest held his head;
The most Accomplish't was esteem'd to be,
Of comely Forme, well-grac't Activity;
The *Muses* too, like him, did none inspire,
None so did stop the Pipe, or touch the Lyre;
Sweet was his Voice, and Eloquent his Tongue;
Alike admired when he Spoke, or Sung!
But these so much Excelling parts the Swain,
With Imperfections no less Great, did stain:

For proud he was, of an Ungovern'd Will,
With Love Familiar, but a Stranger still
To Faith and Constancy; and did his Heart,
Retaining none, expose to ev'ry Dart.
Hapless *Rodanthe*, the Fond Rover, caught,
To whom, for Love, with usual Arts he sought;
Which she, ah too unwary, did bestow :
'Cause True her self, believ'd that he was so.
But he, alas, more wav'ring than the Wind,
Streight broke the Chain, she thought so fast did bind ;
For he no sooner saw her Heart was gain'd,
But he as soon the Victory disdain'd ;
Mad Love else-where, as if 'twere like Renown,
Hearts to subdue, as to take in a Town :
But in the One as Manhood does prevail,
Both Truth and Manhood in the other fail.
And now the Nymph (of late so gay and bright,
The Glory of the Plains and the Delight,
Who still in Wit and Mirth all Pastimes led)
Hung like a wither'd Flow'r her drooping Head.

   I need not tell the Grief *Rodanthe* found,
How all that should asswage, enrag'd her Wound;

Her

Her Form, her Fame, her Vertue, Riches, Wit,
Like Deaths sad Weights upon her Soul did sit:
Or else like Furies stood before her Face,
Still urging and Upbraiding her Disgrace;
In that the World could yield her no Content,
But what alone the False *Alcander* sent.
'Twas said, through just Disdain, at last she broke
The Disingenious and Unworthy Yoke:
But this I know, her Passion held long time,
Constancy, though Unhappy, is no Crime.

Remember when you Love, from that same hour
Your Peace you put into your Lovers Power:
From that same hour from him you Laws receive;
And as he shall ordain, you Joy, or Grieve,
Hope, Fear, Laugh, Weep; Reason aloof does stard;
Disabl'd both to Act, and to Command.
Oh Cruel Fetters! rather wish to feel,
On your soft Limbs, the Gauling Weight of Steel;
Rather to bloudy Wounds oppose your Breast.
No Ill, by which the Body can be prest;
You will so sensible a Torment find,
As Shackles on your captivated Mind.

The Mind from Heaven its high Descent did draw,
And brooks uneasily any other Law,
Than what from Reason dictated shall be,
Reason, a kind of In-mate Deity.
Which only can adapt to ev'ry Soul
A Yoke so fit and light, that the Controle
All Liberty excels; so sweet a Sway,
The same 'tis to be Happy, and Obey;
Commands so Wise and with Rewards so drest
That the according Soul replys, *I'm Blest.*
This teaches rightly how to Love and Hate,
To fear and hope by Measure and just Weight;
What Tears in Grief ought from our Eyes to flow,
What Transport in Felicity to show;
In ev'ry Passion how to steer the Will,
Tho rude the Shock, to keep it steady still.
Oh happy Mind! what words can speak thy Bliss,
When in a Harmony thou mov'st like this?

    Your Hearts fair Virgins keep smooth as your Brow,
Not the least Am'rous Passion there allow;
Hold not a Parly with what may betray
Your inward Freedom to a Forraign Sway;

And

And while thus ore your selves you Queens remain,
Unenvy'd, ore the World, let others reign:
The highest Joy which from Dominion flows,
Is short of what a Mind well-govern'd knows.

 Whither my *Muse*, would'st uncontrouled run?
Contend in Motion with the restless Sun?
Immortal thou, but I a mortal Sire
Exhaust my strength, and Hearers also tire.

 Al. O Heaven-taught Bard! to Ages couldst prolong
Thy Soul-instructing, Health-infusing Song,
I with unweary'd Appetite could hear,
And wish my Senses were turn'd all to Ear.

 Alcim. Old Man, thy frosty Precepts well betray
Thy Blood is cold, and that thy Head is grey:
Who past the Pleasure Love and Youth can give,
To spoyl't in others, now dost only live.
Wouldst thou, indeed, if so thou couldst perswade,
The Fair, whose Charms have many Lovers made,
Should feel Compassion for no one they wound,
But be to all Inexorable found?

 Me. Young man, if my advice thou well hadst weigh'd,
Thou would'st have found, for either Sex 'twas made;

And would from Womens Beauty thee no less
Preserve, than them secure from thy Address.
But let thy Youth thy rash Reproach excuse.

Alci. Fairest *Amira* let him not abuse
Thy gentle Heart, by his imprinting there
His doting Maxims------But I will not fear:
For when 'gainst Love he fiercest did inveigh,
Methoughts I saw thee turn with Scorn away.

Ami. Alcimedon according to his Will
Does all my Words and Looks interpret still:
But I shall learn at length how to Disdain,
Or at the least more cunningly to feign.

Alci. No wonder thou *Alcimedon* art rude,
When with no Gen'rous Quality endu'd:
But hop'st by railing Words Vice to defend,
Which Foulers made, by having such a Friend.

Amira, thou art warn'd, wisely beware,
Leap not with Open-Eyes into the Snare:
The Faith that's given to thee, was given before
To *Nais*, *Amoret*, and many more:
The Perjur'd did the Gods to Witness call,
That unto each he was the only Thrall.

Asteria.

Aste. Y'ave made his Cheeks with Conscious blushes glow.

Alci. 'Tis the best Colour a False Heart can show;
And well it is with Guilt some shame remains.

Meli. Hast, Shepherd, hast to cleanse away thy stains,
Let not thy Youth, of Time the goodly spring,
Neglected pass, that nothing forth it bring
But noxious Weeds: which cultivated might
Produce such Crops, as now would thee delight,
And give thee after Fame: For Vertues Fruit
Believe it, not alone with Age does sute,
Nought adorns Youth like to a Noble Mind,
In thee this Union let *Amira* find.

Lici. O fear her not! she'l serve him in his kind.

Meli. See how Discourse upon the Time does prey,
Those hours pass swiftest, that we talk away.
Declining *Sol* forsaken hath the Fields,
And Mountains highest Summits only gildes:
Which warns us home-wards with our Flocks to make.

Alci. Along with thee our Thanks and Praises take.

Aste. In which our Hearts do all in One unite,

Lici. Our Wishes too, That on thy Head may light,
What e're the Gods as their Best Gifts bestow.

Meli. Kind Nymphs on you may Equal Blessings flow.

L

On my Aunt Mrs A. K.

Drown'd under London-bridge, *in the* QUEENS *Bardge,* Anno 1641.

THe Darling of a Father Good and Wife,
   The Vertue, which a Vertuous Age did prize;
The Beauty Excellent even to thofe were Faire,
Subfcrib'd unto, by fuch as might compare;
The Star that 'bove her Orb did always move,
And yet the Nobleft did not Hate, but Love;
And thofe who moft upon their Title ftood,
Vail'd alfo to, becaufe fhe did more Good.
To whom the Wrong'd, and Worthy did refort,
And held their Sutes obtain'd, if only brought;
The higheft Saint in all the Heav'n of Court.
So Noble was her Aire, fo Great her Meen,
She feem'd a Friend, not Servant to the Queen.
To Sin, if known, fhe never did give way,
Vice could not Storm her, could it not betray.

When

When angry Heav'n extinguisht her fair Light,
It seem'd to say, *Nought's Precious in my sight;
As I in Waves this Paragon have drown'd,
The Nation next, and King I will confound.*

On a young Lady

Whose LORD *was Travelling.*

NO sooner I pronounced *Celindas* name,
But Troops of wing'd Pow'rs did chant the same:
Not those the Poets Bows and Arrows lend,
But such as on the Altar do attend.
Celinda nam'd, Flow'rs spring up from the Ground,
Excited meerly with the Charming Sound.
Celinda, the Courts Glory, and its fear,
The gaz'd at Wonder, where she does appear.
Celinda great in Birth, greater in Meen,
Yet none so humble as this Fair-One's seen.
Her Youth and Beauty justly might disdain,
But the least Pride her Glories ne're did stain.

Celinda

Celinda of each State th'ambitious Strife,
At once a Noble Virgin, and a Wife

 Who, while her Gallant Lord in Forraign parts
Adorns his Youth with all accomplisht Arts,
Grows ripe at home in Vertue, more than Years,
And in each Grace a Miracle appears!

 When other of her Age a madding go,
To th' Park and Plays, and ev'ry publick Show,
Proud from their Parents Bondage they have broke,
Though justly freed, she still does wear the Yoke;
Preferring more her Mothers Friend to be,
Than Idol of the Towns Loose-Gallantry.
On her she to the Temple does attend,
Where they their Blessed Hours both save and spend.
They Smile, they Joy, together they do Pray,
You'd think two Bodies did One Soul obey:
Like Angels thus they do reflect their Bliss,
And their bright Vertues each the other kiss.

 Return young Lord, while thou abroad dost rome
The World to see, thou loosest Heaven at Home.

ON THE
Dutchess of Grafton
Under the Name of ALINDA.
A SONG.

I.

TH'ambitious Eye that seeks alone,
   Where Beauties Wonders most are shown;
Of all that bounteous Heaven displays,
Let him on bright *Alinda* gaze;
And in her high Example see,
All can admir'd, or wisht-for, be!

II.

An unmatch't Form, Mind like endow'd,
Estate, and Title great and proud;
A Charge Heaven dares to few commit,
So few, like her, can manage it;
Without all Blame or Envy bear,
The being Witty, Great and Fair!

III.

So well these Murd'ring Weapons weild,
As first Herself with them to shield,
Then slaughter none in proud Disport,
Destroy those she invites to Court:
Great are her Charmes, but Vertue more,
She wounds no Hearts, though All adore!

IV.

'Tis Am'rous Beauty Love invites,
A Passion, like it self, excites:
The Paragon, though all admire,
Kindles in none a fond desire:
No more than those the Kings Renown
And State applaud, affect his Crown.

*These following **Fragments** among many more were found among her Papers.*

Penelope to Ulysses.

REturn my dearest Lord, at length return,
Let me no longer your sad absence mourn,
Ilium in Dust, does no more Work afford,
No more Employment for your Wit or Sword.

Why did not the fore-seeing Gods destroy,
Helin the Fire-brand both of *Greece* and *Troy*,
E're yet the Fatal Youth her Face had seen,
E're lov'd and born away the wanton Queen?
Then had been stopt the mighty Floud of Woe,
Which now both *Greece* and *Phrygia* over-flow:
Then I, these many Teares, should not have shed,
Nor thou, the source of them, to War been led:
I should not then have trembled at the Fame
Of *Hectors* warlike and victorious Name.

Why

Why did I wish the Noble *Hector* Slain?
Why *Ilium* ruin'd? Rise, O rise again!
Again great City flourish from thine Urne:
For though thou'rt burn'd, my Lord does not return.
Sometimes I think, (but O most Cruel Thought,)
That, for thy Absence, th'art thy self in fault:
That thou art captiv'd by some captive Dame,
Who, when thou fired'st *Troy*, did thee inflame
And now with her thou lead'st thy am'rous Life,
Forgetful, and despising of thy Wife.

An Epitaph on her Self.

When I am Dead, few Friends attend my Hearse,
And for a Monument, I leave my VERSE.

An ODE.

Arise my Dove, from mid'st of Pots arise,
    Thy sully'd Habitation leave,
      To Dust no longer cleave,
Unworthy they of Heaven, that will not view the Skies.

Thy native Beauty re-assume,
 Prune each neglected Plume,
 Till more than Silver white,
 Then burnisht Gold more bright,
Thus ever ready stand to take thy Eternal Flight.

II.
The Bird to whom the spacious Aire was given,
As in a smooth and trackless Path to go,
 A Walk which does no Limits know
 Pervious alone to Her and Heaven:
 Should she her Airy Race forget,
 On Earth affect to walk and sit ;
Should she so high a Priviledge neglect,
As still on Earth, to walk and sit, affect,
 What could she of Wrong complain,
 Who thus her Birdly Kind doth stain,
 If all her Feathers moulted were,
 And naked she were left and bare,
 The Jest and Scorn of Earth and Aire?

III.
The Bird of Paradice the Soul,

M

Extem-

Extemporary Counsel given to a Young Gallant *in a* Frolick.

AS you are Young, if you'l be also Wise,
Danger with Honour court, ~~Quarrels~~ *but broils* despise;

Believe you then are truly Brave and Bold,

To Beauty when no Slave, and less to Gold;

When Vertue you dare own, not think it odd,

Or ungenteel to say, *I fear a God.*

These Three following O D E S being found among Mrs Killigrews *Papers, I was willing to Print though none of hers.*

CLO-

Cloris Charmes

Dissolved by EUDORA.

I.

NOt that thy Fair Hand
  Should lead me from my deep Dispaire,
Or thy Love, *Cloris*, End my Care,
  And back my Steps command:
But if hereafter thou Retire,
To quench with Tears, thy Wandring Fire,
  This Clue I'll leave behinde,
  By which thou maist untwine
    The Saddest Way,
    To shun the Day,
  That ever Grief did find.

II.
First take thy Hapless Way
Along the Rocky Northern Shore,
Infamous for the Matchless Store
   Of Wracks within that Bay.
None o're the Cursed Beach e're crost,
Unless the Robb'd, the Wrack'd, or Lost
   Where on the Strand lye spread,
   The Sculls of many Dead.
     Their mingl'd Bones,
     Among the Stones,
Thy Wretched Feet must tread.

III.
The Trees along the Coast,
Stretch forth to Heaven their blasted Arms,
As if they plaind the North-winds harms,
   And Youthful Verdure lost.
There stands a Grove of Fatal Ewe,
Where Sun nere pierc't, nor Wind ere blew.
   In it a Brooke doth fleet,
   The Noise must guide thy Feet,

For

For there's no Light,
But all is Night,
And Darkness that you meet.

IV.

Follow th'Infernal Wave,
Until it spread into a Floud,
Poysoning the Creatures of the Wood,
There twice a day a Slave,
I know not for what Impious Thing,
Bears thence the Liquor of that Spring.
It adds to the sad Place,
To hear how at each Pace,
He curses God,
Himself, his Load,
For such his Forlorn Case.

V.

Next make no Noyse, nor talk,
Until th'art past a Narrow Glade,
Where Light does only break the Shade;
'Tis a Murderers Walk.
Observing this thou need'st not fear,
He sleeps the Day or Wakes elsewhere.

Though

Though there's no Clock or Chime,

The Hour he did his Crime,

    His Soul awakes,

    His Conscience quakes

And warns him that's the Time.

VI.

Thy Steps must next advance,

Where Horrour, Sin, and Spectars dwell,

Where the Woods Shade seems turn'd Hell,

    Witches here Nightly Dance,

And Sprights joyn with them when they call,

The Murderer dares not view the Ball.

    For Snakes and Toads conspire,

    To make them up a Quire.

        And for their Light,

        And Torches bright,

    The Fiends dance all on fire.

VII.

Press on till thou descrie

Among the Trees sad, gastly, wan,

Thinne as the Shadow of a Man,

    One that does ever crie,

She

She is not; and she ne're will be,
Despair and Death come swallow me,
    Leave him; and keep thy way,
    No more thou now canst stray
        Thy Feet do stand,
        In Sorrows Land,
    It's Kingdomes every way.

VIII.

Here Gloomy Light will shew
Rear'd like a Castle to the Skie,
A Horrid Cliffe there standing nigh
    Shading a Creek below.
In which Recess there lies a Cave,
Dreadful as Hell, still as the Grave.
    Sea-Monsters there abide,
    The coming of the Tide,
        No Noise is near,
        To make them fear,
God-sleep might there reside.

IX.

But when the Boysterous Seas,
With Roaring Waves resumes this Cell,
You'd swear the Thunders there did dwell.

So lowd he makes his Plea;
So Tempests bellow under ground,
And Ecchos multiply the Sound!

This is the place I chose,
Changeable like my Woes,
Now calmly Sad,
Then Raging Mad,
As move my Bitter Throwes.

X.

Such Dread besets this Part,
That all the Horrour thou hast past,
Are but Degrees to This at last.

The sight must break thy Heart:
Here Bats and Owles that hate the Light,
Fly and enjoy Eternal Night.

Scales of Serpents, Fish-bones,
Th'Adders Eye, and Toad-stones,
Are all the Light,
Hath blest my Sight,
Since first began my Groans.

XI.

XI.

When thus I lost the Sense,
Of all the heathful World calls Bliss,
And held it Joy, those Joys to miss,
    When Beauty was Offence:
Celestial Strains did read the Aire,
Shaking these Mansions of Despaire;
    A Form Divine and bright,
    Stroke Day through all that Night
        As when Heav'ns Queen
        In Hell was seen,
    With wonder and affright!

XII.

The Monsters fled for fear,
The Terrors of the Cursed Wood
Dismantl'd were, and where they stood,
    No longer did appear.
The Gentle Pow'r, which wrought this thing,
Eudora was, who thus did sing.
    Dissolv'd is Cloris *spell,*
    From whence thy Evils fell,
        Send her this Clue,
        'Tis there most due
    And thy Phantastick Hell.

Upon a Little Lady

Under the Discipline of an Excellent Person.

I.

How comes the Day orecast ? the Flaming Sun
Darkn'd at Noon, as if his Course were run?
He never rose more proud, more glad, more gay,
Ne're courted *Daphne* with a brighter Ray!
  And now in Clouds he wraps his Head,
As if not *Daphne*, but himself were dead!
    And all the little Winged Troop
    Forbear to sing, and sit and droop;
    The Flowers do languish on their Beds,
    And fading hang their Mourning Heads;
    The little *Cupids* discontented, shew,
    In Grief and Rage one breaks his Bow,
    An other tares his Cheeks and Haire,
A third sits blubring in Despaire,

Confessing though, in Love, he be,
A Powerful, Dreadful Deitie,
A Child, in Wrath, can do as much as he!
Whence is this Evil hurl'd,
On all the sweetness of the World?
Among those Things with Beauty shine,
(Both Humane natures, and Divine)
There was not so much sorrow spi'd,
No, not that Day the sweet *Adonis* died!

II.

Ambitious both to know the Ill, and to partake,
The little Weeping Gods I thus bespake.
Ye Noblest Pow'rs and Gentlest that Above,
Govern us Men, but govern still with Love,
Vouchsafe to tell, what can that Sorrow be,
Disorders Heaven, and wounds a Deitie.
My Prayer not spoken out,
One of the Winged Rout,
With Indignation great,
Sprung from his Airie-Seat,
And mounting to a Higher Cloud,
With Thunder, or a Voice as loud

Cried

Cried, Mortal there, there seek the Grief o'th'Gods,
Where thou findst Plagues, and their revengeful Rods!
   And in the Instant that the Thing was meant,
He bent his Bow, his Arrow plac't, and to the mark it sent!
   I follow'd with my watchful Eye,
   To the Place where the Shaft did flie,
   But O unheard-of Prodigy.
   It was retorted back again,
   And he that sent it, felt the pain,
Alas! I think the little God was therewith slain!
   But wanton Darts ne're pierce where Honours found,
   And those that shoot them, do their own Breasts wound.

III.

The Place from which the Arrow did return,
Swifter then sent, and with the speed did burn,
Was a Proud Pile which Marble Columnes bare,
Tarrast beneath, and open to the Aire,
On either side, Cords of wove Gold did tie
A purfl'd Curtain, hanging from on high,
To clear the Prospect of the stately Bower,
And boast the Owners Dignity and Power!
   This shew'd the Scene from whence Loves grief arose,
And Heaven and Nature both did discompose,

A little Nymph whoſe Limbs divinely bright,

Lay like a Body of Collected Light,

But not to Love and Courtſhip ſo diſclos'd,

But to the Rigour of a Dame oppos'd,

Who inſtant on the Faire with Words and Blows,

Now chaſtens Error, and now Virtue ſhews.

IV.

But O thou no leſs Blind,

Than Wild and Savage Mind,

Who Diſcipline dar'ſt name,

Thy Outrage and thy ſhame,

And hop'ſt a Radiant Crown to get

All Stars and Glory to thy Head made fit,

Know that this Curſe alone ſhall Serpent-like incircle it!

May'ſt thou henceforth, be ever ſeen to ſtand,

Graſping a Scourge of Vipers in thy Hand,

Thy Hand, that Furie like——But ſee!

By *Apollos* Sacred Tree,

By his ever Tuneful Lyre,

And his bright Image the Eternal Fire,

Eudoras ſhe has done this Deed

And made the World thus in its Darling bleed!

I know the Cruel Dame,
Too well inſtructed by my Flame!
But ſee her ſhape! But ſee her Face!
In her Temple ſuch is *Diana*'s Grace!
Behold her Lute upon the Pavement lies,
When Beautie's wrong'd, no wonder Muſick dies!

V.

What blood of *Centaurs* did thy Boſom warme,
And boyle the Balſome there up to a Storme?
Nay Balſome flow'd not with ſo ſoft a Floud,
As thy Thoughts Evenly Virtuous, Mildly Good!
How could thy Skilful and Harmonious Hand,
That Rage of Seas, and People could command,
And calme Diſeaſes with the Charming ſtrings,
Such Diſcords make in the whole Name of Things?

But now I ſee the Root of thy Raſh Pride,
Becauſe thou didſt Excel the World beſide,
And it in Beauty and in Fame out-ſhine,
Thou would'ſt compare thy ſelf to things Divine!
And 'bove thy Standard what thou there didſt ſee,
Thou didſt Condemn, becauſe 'twas unlike thee,
And puniſht in the Lady as unfit,
What Bloomings were of a Diviner Wit.

Divine

Divine she is, or else Divine must be,
A Borne or else a Growing Deitie!

VI.
    While thus I did exclaime,
    And wildly rage and blame,
    Behold the *Sylvan*-Quire
    Did all at one conspire,
    With shrill and cheerful Throats,
    T'assume their chirping Notes;
    The Heav'ns refulgent Eye
    Dance't in the clear'd-up Skie,
    And so triumphant shon,
  As seven-days Beams he had on!
The little Loves burn'd with Nobler Fire,
Each chang'd his wanton Bow, and took a Lyre,
Singing chast Aires unto the tuneful strings,
And time'd soft Musick with their downy Wings.

    I turn'd the little Nymph to view,
    She singing and did smiling shew;
    Eudora led a heav'nly strain,
Her Angels Voice did escho it again!

I then decreed no Sacriledge was wrought,
But neerer Heav'n this Piece of Heaven was brought.
She also brighter seem'd, than she had been,
Vertue darts forth a Light'ning 'bove the Skin.
Eudora also shew'd as heretofore,
When her soft Graces I did first adore.

    I saw, what one did *Nobly Will*,

    The other *sweetly did fulfil*;

Their Actions all harmoniously did sute,
And she had only tun'd the Lady like her Lute.

On the Soft and Gentle
Motions of Eudora.

Divine *Thalia* strike th'Harmonious Lute,
But with a Stroke so Gentle as may sute
The silent gliding of the Howers,
Or yet the calmer growth of Flowers;
Th'ascending or the falling Dew,
Which none can see, though all find true.
    For thus alone,
    Can be shewn,
  How downie, how smooth,
  Eudora doth Move,
How Silken her Actions appear,
    The Aire of her Face,
    Of a gentler Grace
Then those that do stroke the Eare.
  Her Address so sweet,
  So Modestly Meet,

That 'tis not the Lowd though Tuneable String,
Can shewforth so soft, so Noyseless a Thing!
O This to express from thy Hand must fall,
Then Musicks self, something more Musical.

FINIS.

ERRATA.

IN Mr. *Drydens* Ode, Stanzo 5. at the end of the first line read [None.] p. 9. v. 6. for her r. its. p. 24. v. 1. for renown'd r. renowned. p. 38. v. last but one, for renounced r. renowned. p. 57. v. 1. instead of the Interrogation-point, make a Comma. p. 97. v. 13. r. burn'd with a nobler fier.

THE TABLE.

Alexandreis.	Page 1
To the *Queen*.	6
A Pastoral Dialogue.	11
On Death.	13
First Epigram, *Upon being contended with a Little*.	15
The Second Epigram, *On Billinda*.	ibid.
The Third Epigram, *On an Atheist*.	16
The Fourth Epigram, *On Galla*.	17
A Farewel to Worldly Joys.	18
The Complaint of a Lover.	19
Love, the Soul of Poetry.	22
To my Lady Berkley, *Afflicted upon her Son my Lord* Berkley's *early Engaging in the Sea-Service*.	24
St. John *Baptist Painted by her Self in the Wilderness, with Angels appearing to him, and with a Lamb by him*.	27
Herodias's *Daughter presenting to her Mother St. Johns Head in a Silver Charger, also Painted by her self*.	ibid.
On a Picture Painted by her self, *representing two Nymphs of* Diana's, *one in a posture to Hunt, the other Batheing*.	28
An Invective against Gold.	30
The Miseries of Man.	32
Upon the saying that my Verses were made by another.	44
On the Birth-Day of Queen Katherine.	47

The TABLE.

To my Lord Colrane, in Answer to his Complemental Verses sent me under the Name of Cleanor.	49
The Discontent.	51
A Pastoral Dialogue.	57
A Pastoral Dialogue.	63
On my Aunt Mrs. A. K. drowned under London-Bridge in the Queens Barge, 1641.	76
On a young Lady, whose Lord was Travelling.	77
On the Dutchess of Grafton, under the Name of Allinda, a Song.	79
Penelope to Ulysses.	81
An Epitaph on her Self.	82
An Ode.	ibid.
Extemporary Counsel, given to a young Gallant in a Frolick.	84
Cloris Charms Dissolv'd by Eudora.	85
Upon a Little Lady under the Discipline of an Excellent Person.	92
On the soft and gentle motions of Eudora.	99